CW01524181

MORAL COURAGE

MORAL COURAGE

19 Profiles of Investigative Journalists

Anthony Feinstein

G Editions  New York

First published in 2023 by

G Editions
www.geditions.com
media@geditions.com

First edition, 2023

Library of Congress Cataloging-in-Publication data is available
from the publisher.

Hardcover edition
ISBN: 978-1-943876-41-9

Printed and bound in the United States of America

10 9 8 7 6 5 4 3 2 1

To Diane Foley

"Life is mostly froth and bubble,
Two things stand like stone,
Kindness in another's trouble,
Courage in your own."

—Adam Lindsay Gordon

Contents

Introduction 15

IRAN

Mohammad
Mosaed

57

INDIA

Neha Dixit

69

RUSSIA

David Frenkel

83

CZECH REPUBLIC AND SLOVAKIA
Pavla Holcová

SERBIA
Stevan Dojčinović

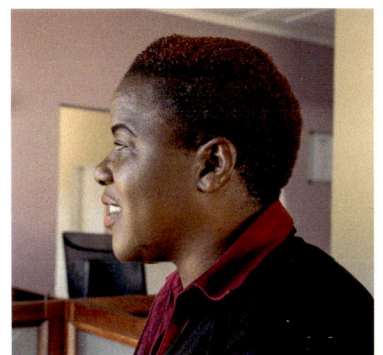

ZAMBIA
Mwape Kumwenda

Anthony Feinstein

This book grew out of a series of twelve articles that I wrote for the *Globe and Mail* in Canada in which I individually profiled journalists who have shown remarkable courage continuing their work in the face of danger. I needed to understand why these journalists remain so committed to their profession despite the grave risks this entails.

I began my inquiry by focusing on countries that have very poor records of freedom of the press. Russia, Belarus, Iran, Syria, Bangladesh, Afghanistan, Myanmar, Azerbaijan, and Zimbabwe are consistently near the bottom of the list in Reporters Without Borders' annual global index of press freedom. Other countries, like India and Turkey, are rapidly slipping down into the murky depths as well. What all these countries share is an intolerance of a free press. Journalists who tell an inconvenient truth are treated brutally.

The first part of my theory is that the dedication of these journalists can be explained by a key attribute: moral courage. Motivation is more complex than encompassing a single factor, of course. But when the consequences of investigative reporting include vicious harassment, death threats, beatings, torture, mock execution, prolonged imprisonment and death, an extraordinary moral courage is required to endure and continue working.

The second part is that moral courage is essential if moral injury is to be kept at bay. Moral courage and moral injury are therefore inextricably bound to one another. This symbiotic relationship comes into clearer focus if we start with a definition of what moral injury is. This refers to a condition that arises from witnessing, perpetrating, or failing to prevent acts that transgress a person's code of ethics or moral compass. The definition indicates that moral injury may occur in response to something a person does, an act of commission, or fails to do, an act of omission. It is typically associated with feelings of shame, guilt, anger, and disgust. Moral courage translated into action may therefore be seen as the antidote, as it were, to these distressing emotions.

Having defined moral injury, an explanation of what moral courage entails is also needed. The ancient Greeks defined the moral dimensions of character according to virtues and vices. To Plato, virtue comprises practical wisdom, moral courage, justice, and temperance. While his concepts were influenced by Athenian philosophy, it is notable that when the cultural bandwidth is expanded to include Confu-

cianism, Daoism, Buddhism, Hinduism, Christianity, Judaism, and Islam, courage remains as one of six virtues—the others being justice, humanity, temperance, wisdom, and transcendence.

Delving further into what defines courage, four components have been identified: bravery, industry, honesty, and vitality.* These attributes are considered integral to individuals achieving their goals when faced with opposition that can be external (for example, governments jailing journalists) or internal (journalists' fear of imprisonment).

On top of these basic building blocks are other characterological traits identified by behavioral scientists in those individuals who show moral courage. They include, among others, high self-esteem, confidence in one's judgment and values, a strong sense of social responsibility, higher levels of independence, compassion, empathy, altruism, extraversion, non-conform-

---

* Dahlsgaard K, Peterson C, Seligman M. "Shared virtue: The convergence of valued human strengths across culture and history." *Review of General Psychology*, 2005, 9(3), 203-213.

ism, and proclivity for risk-taking. Some of these behavioral traits can be learned, while others are more innate. Parents, role models, and mentors can have a profound influence in determining how individuals set their moral compass.

Rushworth Kidder (2005)* utilizes a simple Venn diagram to illustrates three necessary components that must be present to manifest moral courage. The first component is principles, the second is endurance (best conceptualized as the will to act), and the third, danger. Moral courage is to be found where all three circles intersect. He goes on to show that having only two components falls short in various ways. For example, principles without endurance in the presence of danger leads to timidity; the presence of danger and endurance without principles is indicative of physical courage only; and principles and endurance without a proper apprecia-

tion of danger can be seen as foolhardiness.

All human behavior and emotion lie along a continuum ranging from minimal to marked, or negligible to extreme, depending on the descriptors used. The same is true for moral injury with its attendant emotions, and moral courage. This continuum follows the shape of a bell curve, meaning that most individuals clump together in their shared beliefs and emotions. Everyone has a moral compass with a threshold for determining what constitutes egregious behavior. This, too, will vary across the spectrum and follows a bell curve distribution. When that threshold is transgressed, uncomfortable emotions like guilt and disgust are elicited. Not everyone, however, will speak out or do something when their threshold is infringed. Understandably, as the consequences of responding to morally egregious behavior become increasingly more hazardous, the

---

* Readers wanting to learn more on the subject of moral courage are directed to *Moral Courage* by Rushworth Kidder (William Morrow, 2005), *The Quest for Character* by Masimo Pigliucci (Basic Books, 2022), *Why We Act: Turning Bystanders into Moral Rebels* by Catherine Sanderson (The Belknap Press of Harvard University Press, 2020), and *On Moral Courage* by Compton MacKenzie (Collins, 1962).

number of people prepared to say something or take action becomes very small indeed. The journalists who are featured in this book all fit into this very small, select group. The niche they occupy is at the far end of the bell curve.

As my book reveals, these journalists have not arrived at this rarefied place solely by chance. Moral courage, a component of free will, has led them there. And one of the most remarkable aspects to their journey is this: despite the grave threats and violence endured, notwithstanding the grievous losses sustained and the fear experienced, these journalists would rather occupy this select spot on the moral courage spectrum than keep quiet. In countries like Russia, Belarus, Bangladesh, and Iran, among many others, it has fallen to them to keep alive the remnants of their failing civil societies. In doing so, they remind their fellow citizens, cowed by authoritarian governments or criminal gangs, that all may not be lost.

Lister in the garden of the Kelvin Grove Club, before addressing the Cape Town Press Club.
Cape Town, South Africa.

Gwen Lister

In her autobiography, *Comrade Editor*, Gwen Lister writes, "Just before I reached my teens, apartheid hit me right between the eyes." This political awakening is no mere abstraction, for it is soon followed by action. The year is 1966. Life in South Africa is defined by the color of one's skin. Thirteen-year-old Gwen is traveling on a double-decker bus in Cape Town. In keeping with the country's punitive laws ensuring strict racial segregation, the seats on the upper level are reserved for Black people while white people must sit below. An elderly black woman gets on the bus, laden with parcels. What happens next is best left to Lister to describe.

"I see she won't make it up the stairs, and so I get up to give her my seat. She takes it and white passengers explode with abuse towards both of us. The hurt in her eyes strikes me like a bolt of lightning. In that instant, my life changed irrevocably, my conscience was fully awakened, and my passion ignited. I resolved never again to remain silent in the face of injustice in general and the oppressive reality of apartheid in particular."

Let us pause and examine what she has written. First, there is the language, which is forceful, direct, unequivocal. "Hit between the eyes," "struck like a bolt of lightning"—descriptors like these leave the reader in no doubt as to the gravitas of what has taken place. Language, however, is only the messenger. It is the message that is more remarkable by far, for it is coming from a young girl whose moral compass has been already set. Can a thirteen-year-old resolve never to remain silent in the face of injustice and then hold herself to that

Above: *An attendee at the book signing for Lister's autobiography,* Comrade Editor: On Life, Journalism, and the Birth of Namibia.

The author in discussion with attendees at her talk at the Cape Town Press Club.

high bar over the course of half a century?

In Lister's case, the answer is yes. What the child could not know at the time was the career path that would give her the means, in a very public and influential way, to follow the high moral ground. A precocious sensibility thankfully does not include clairvoyance, as the struggle that lay in wait would prove supremely taxing.

The year of Lister's "a-ha moment," 1966, also saw the assassination of Hendrik Verwoerd, the prime minister of South Africa and the ideological architect of apartheid. Verwoerd's stabbing in Parliament shocked the nation but never shifted the granite resolve of his Nationalist Party. This meant that by the time Lister graduated with her bachelor of arts degree from the University of Cape Town, racial segregation remained deeply entrenched in South African society.

While she was impatient to help dismantle it, Lister also rejected violence and did not join Umkhonto we Sizwe, the armed wing of Nelson Mandela's banned African National Congress. Instead, she settled on journalism and applied for a vacant position at the *Windhoek Advertiser*, a daily newspaper in the neighboring territory of South West Africa, now known as Namibia. A former German colony, South West Africa had been placed under South African administration by the League of Nations after the First World War. Despite the United Nations revoking this mandate in 1966, South Africa continued to govern the country.

To Lister, a move to the territory was strategic and practical. Imbued with a strong sense of urgency, she reasoned that if apartheid was to be defeated, it would occur first in a mandated territory like South West Africa, rather than in South Africa, its ideological home. And if her contribution to achieving this would be through journalism, obtaining her own political column with a beginner's résumé would be easier and quicker in South West Africa than in South Africa—where the only position open to her was that of cub reporter.

She arrived at the *Advertiser* mid-morning for her interview to find the editor,

Johannes Marthinus Smith, known by all as Smittie, already drunk. "Women belong barefoot in the kitchen or naked in bed," he yelled at her. Recounting this episode in her autobiography, Lister writes with remarkable restraint that she had "never come across someone like him before." It says much for her strength of character that she not only withstood the abuse, but was hired by Jurgen Meinert, the paper's owner, despite Smittie's chauvinistic objections. She soon learned that behind the editor's bullying bluster was a fiercely independent journalist, prepared to stand firm against the pressures being exerted on the *Advertiser* by the South African government. In time, an unlikely friendship would develop between the two.

Lister was moving to a country roiled by racial tensions. The South West African's People's Organization (SWAPO), considered by the United Nations as the sole legitimate representative of the Namibian people, had taken up arms against the occupying South African military. Compounding the situation, neighboring and newly independent Angola was being torn apart in a civil war fueled by Cold War enmities that saw the Soviet Union and her Cuban proxies locked in battle with U.S.-backed South Africa. Against this backdrop of superpower rivalries and local internecine feuds, the South African administration was working assiduously to undermine SWAPO and exclude it from the political discourse—a policy that the *Windhoek Advertiser* strongly criticized.

Smittie, despite his misogynistic misgivings, threw Lister into the deep end of Namibian politics. Her first political assignment was a SWAPO rally in Katutura, a racially segregated district reserved for Black people, outside Windhoek. The name *Katutura* in the Herero language means "the place where people do not want to live"—a poignant encapsulation of what apartheid had brought to Namibia. In her memoirs, Lister remembers the rallies as "intimidating experiences . . . massive gatherings which often ended in violence as police would move in to tyrannize the attendees and disperse the crowds."

Lister's sympathetic coverage of SWAPO policies did not fit with the government's narrative of demonizing the organization. The *Advertiser* was censored, and when that heavy-handed approach could not silence her voice, the government used a slush fund to buy out the paper and ensure the new owners followed the prescribed script. Smittie and Lister were given an ultimatum to do likewise. Smittie's response was to resign and use his savings to start a new paper, the *Windhoek Observer*. It was a gamble, and he took Lister with him. Their venture launched on May 4, 1978, the day South African forces attacked SWAPO's Cassinga Camp in southern Angola, killing six hundred people, many of whom were refugees.

The escalating armed conflict was accompanied by more stringent media restrictions, which included revoking Lister's military accreditation. Her home was searched by security police. She was increasingly shunned by the white population in Namibia who regarded her as a "dangerous communist." Her social circle dwindled to a handful of colleagues and a few progressive lawyers. People would cross the street to avoid her. She was mocked and caricatured in cartoons in government-friendly papers. On her return to Namibia from a 1983 United Nations–sponsored conference in Paris in support of Namibian independence, where she met SWAPO's exiled leader Sam Nujoma for the first time, she was charged under the Publications and Customs and Excise Acts and the dreaded Internal Security Act. She faced up to twenty years in jail. Her crime? Having SWAPO publications in her possession.

Lister's trial was held in South Africa. The fear of a guilty verdict and a jail term, and the effect it would have on her three-year-old son, weighed heavily on her. A stellar legal team ensured her acquittal. But there was no letup in the harassment. Single editions of the *Observer* were banned followed by a total ban on the paper in 1984. Smittie was ready to quit, but Lister, with funding from the U.S.-based Lawyers' Committee for Civil Rights Under Law, traveled to South Africa and had the ban overturned.

Politics, however, influenced the purse strings, and the *Observer*'s political stance had driven away advertising revenue from the predominantly white business sector. With the paper in severe financial trouble, Smittie decided to adopt a more moderate political stance. To bolster finances, he also brought on board a wealthy real estate agent, Thurstan Salt, who had aggressively importuned Lister for sex in the past. A knee to the groin had made a vindictive enemy. She was removed from her political beat. Nine staff members of the paper resigned in protest. Lister joined them.

Three months after leaving the *Observer*, Lister was arrested under the Official Secrets Act and briefly jailed for exposing mail tampering by the government. While the case against her soon collapsed, she had reached a professional and personal nadir. She was out of regular work. She and her former *Observer* colleagues were blacklisted by the government, which meant local jobs were not open to them. She had very little money. She was dependent on Bishop James Kauluma of the Anglican Diocese of Namibia for a low-rent house. And her husband had walked out on her. It would be the first of two failed marriages. She believes both husbands had been attracted to her for who she was, but once married, they could not adjust to the pressures that came with it.

The adversities Lister had had to contend with thus far steeled her for what came next. With the help of donors, she started a new paper, the *Namibian*, employing ex-*Observer* colleagues. The paper was established as a not-for-profit Trust, the first of its kind in Africa. It belonged to the public it served, immune to outside commercial interests, a fate that had undermined Smittie's *Observer*. The first edition hit the stands on August 30, 1985.

She now had editorial freedom but that also meant she was more firmly in the crosshairs of a belligerent government. She knew that late-night calls generally meant death threats, but what if they were work-related? She was so pivotal to the fledgling paper's survival that the ringing couldn't be ignored. New dangers

Lister's autobiography is a testament to her role in the establishment of a democratic Namibia, free from the yolk of apartheid.

surfaced, as well. The paper's offices were firebombed. The bomb-proof glass that was installed was soon bullet-scarred. Tear gas was placed in the air conditioning. A triple grenade attack, which included phosphorous, destroyed the office and most of the equipment.

When I asked Lister how she coped with it all, she told me she was too busy fighting battles to allow time for her emotions to get in the way. "I did not have time to say, I am hurt, I am afraid," she said. Given the magnitude of the struggle, she regarded introspection "as something of a luxury." She would go to bed wondering if a hand grenade would be lobbed into her garden. As a result, she slept brokenly, peeping through the curtains on the lookout for assailants. "I became used to it," she told me. "They would not get me down; they were the cowards."

And then there was the gender factor. In the deeply patriarchal society, a woman's character was smeared as soon as she showed independence. "I had to forget I was a woman. I could not let myself give in to my emotions, what people called 'women things,'" she divulged. "I could not show weakness as a woman!"

An intense commitment to a cause generates its own gravitational pull. "The deeper I was in, the harder it was to give up," Lister recalled. "Threats had a paradoxical effect." She asked herself if she was prepared to die, and her answer was yes. "If it had to be, it had to be," she concluded, but she had hoped that those threatening her would have a conscience and spare her children.

When her friend Anton Lubowski, a charismatic lawyer and SWAPO supporter, was assassinated outside his home, a man calling himself White Wolf telephoned the *Namibian* with a chilling message: "Tell Gwen Lister she's next." To Lister, the murder, emotionally devastating, added another layer to her resolve: "Now there were less of us," she recollected, "just a handful of whites opposed to the government. Our work became even more important."

"The most perilous moment for a bad

government is one when it seeks to mend its ways," observed Alexis de Tocqueville. Lubowski was killed three days before the South African government relented and sanctioned Nujoma's return to Namibia after thirty-nine years in exile. Five months later, Namibia was independent with a democratically elected SWAPO government led by Nujoma as president. At long last, Lister could openly let go some of her emotions. She "wept unashamedly" as the Namibian flag was raised just after midnight on March 21, 1990.

But the story does not end here, although it could have with a lesser person. The political transition vindicated Lister's belief that "really good journalism" was defined by its ability to bring about change. To the victors go the spoils of war, and the new SWAPO government came calling bearing gifts. She was offered the post of Minister of Information and Broadcasting. She declined—as she did for other offers, including ambassadorial posts in Sweden and the United Kingdom and director general of the Namibian Broadcasting Corpo-

ration. From then on, President Nujoma and some in SWAPO viewed her with suspicion. They could not understand her refusal, which was driven by her conviction that "for a journalist to be feted in the halls of power meant you were too close to where you shouldn't be."

It may come as a surprise to realize that Lister was only thirty-seven years of age when Namibia became independent. Having kept her distance from SWAPO, she could hold the government and an increasingly authoritarian president accountable for their failings. When they attacked her for her criticism, she felt vindicated. At a 2003 UNESCO-sponsored seminar, she was one of the architects of the Windhoek Declaration, which enshrined a free press as an essential pillar of democracy. Today, Namibia ranks first in Africa for press freedom.

In 2011, Lister stood down as editor of the *Namibian*. "I felt I had amputated one of my limbs," she told me. The intensity of this reaction may be understood in the context of another admission: that she reacts better under fire than to compliments. So, mindful of her sensitivities, I will shy away from encomiums and let the facts speak for themselves. What a story they tell.

They also beg a question, put to her by Ismail Mahomed, former chief justice of South Africa and Namibia: "What made a little white girl like you do what you did?"

"Stunned" by the question, Lister struggled to answer it other than to say it came from deep within her.

So, let us return to that fateful bus ride in Cape Town, half a century ago, the year the architect of apartheid is knifed to death in Parliament. A child witnesses the humiliation of an elderly Black woman and is morally outraged. That indefinable thing she alludes to deep within her is her moral code that has been transgressed. Doing nothing other than give up a seat on a bus in response to this morally injurious event would be an act of omission that only exacerbates the shame, guilt, and anger that apartheid and other forms of injustice foster. A fierce moral courage

is needed to assuage these emotions—one that must surmount being vilified, ostracized, firebombed, denigrated as a woman, and feeling the pain of loss from a close friend's assassination and two marriages that could not survive the vortex of a liberation struggle.

This precis of Gwen Lister's life is, however, incomplete. It fails to acknowledge the sunlit uplands of moral courage reached by a temperament that does indeed thrive under fire. For she has raised two children as a single mother, forged intense bonds of lifelong friendships amid shared adversity, started and sustained a newspaper that played a pivotal role in ending apartheid in South West Africa and the birth of Namibia, and laid the foundations for a free press that nourishes her country's democracy.

There it is: the balance sheet of an extraordinary life, the pain of moral injury and rewards of moral courage laid out, the debit and credit columns interacting synergistically, the spur to action. And the answer to the chief justice's probing question.

Above and right: *Khalvatgar at the Tommy Douglas Burnaby Public Library where he organizes English classes for Afghan women who are new to Canada or who have not had an opportunity to learn English. British Columbia, Canada.*

Abdul Mujeeb Khalvatgar

The Afghan journalist Abdul Mujeeb Khalvatgar is forty-seven years old. He has lived his entire life against the backdrop of violence and conflict; coup, revolution, invasion, foreign occupation, insurrection, civil war, he has seen them all. Twice forced into hurried exile, his life reflects the turbulent history of his country. That he chose journalism for a career gave him more than a ringside seat to some of these bloody events. It placed him firmly in the crosshairs of the current architects of Afghanistan's agony.

Important milestones in Khalvatgar's life mirror pivotal events in Afghanistan's history. He was born in 1973, the year Mohammed Zahir Shah, the last king of Afghanistan, was overthrown in a coup. Young Mujeeb began school in 1979, the year the Russians invaded the country to prop up the Marxist-Leninist agenda of Hafizullah Amin's People's Democratic Party of Afghanistan. To avoid military conscription at the end of his secondary schooling, he enrolled in university hoping to study journalism. His career choice was however dashed by a combination of Soviet-style bureaucratic rigidity and his excellent grades. Students who did well in math and science were channeled into engineering. Free choice did not sit comfortably with the prevailing zeitgeist at the time, be it Afghan or that of their Soviet overlords. As an example of how far and fast Russian influence had inserted itself into Afghan society by then, Khalvatgar's engineering studies at Kabul Polytechnic University entailed a mandatory Russian language course.

With the university seen as a symbol of

the hated Russian occupation, it became a target for the mujahedeen waging a bloody resistance with covert American and Saudi support. Rockets rained down on the campus at regular intervals, classes were suspended, and Khalvatgar's graduation was delayed by eighteen months. By the time he completed his studies, the Russians had been defeated, civil war raged, and the Taliban were on the rise. When they seized power in 1996, Khalvatgar slipped across the border into Iran abetted by human smugglers. His first period of exile had begun.

Khalvatgar worked in construction in Tehran for four years, an undocumented refugee using his Soviet-acquired engineering skills to get by. After the attacks of September 11, 2001, and the subsequent rout of the Taliban by Western coalition forces, he returned home and began working for the Kabul Afghanistan Reconstruction Agency. He resigned after a year, appalled by the Agency's corruption.

Given Afghanistan's tragic denouement, it is easy to forget that the early years following the defeat of the Taliban were filled with optimism and hope. A rare opportunity to build a free and democratic civil society presented itself under the protective umbrella of Western firepower and munificence. It was a time of enormous flux and change and, to Khalvatgar, an opportunity to reinvent himself by rekindling career hopes that had been quashed by suffocating pseudo-academic diktats. He began training as a journalist.

Freedom can be liberating. And liberty can be energizing. You can readily sense this from the twenty-seven-year-old, newly married Khalvatgar as he plunged hungrily into the myriad opportunities presenting themselves. Internews, an international nonprofit organization supporting independent media by training journalists and digital right activists, established an office in Kabul in 2002. The group hired Khalvatgar as a journalist assistant. He attended the courses they and Radio Free Europe offered. At the same time, he returned to Kabul University to study Farsi literature but switched track to complete a bachelor of arts degree in political science. This was

Khakvatgar and his Afghan-Canadian students.

followed by a two-year master's degree in international relations from Kateb University, a private university in Kabul founded in 2007. All the while, he continued working after hours for Internews, moving up the ladder from assistant to running a news program called *Be Informed* to managing the entire radio station.

When Internews established an Afghan version of their model, the Afghan journalists involved suggested it be called Nai, the name denoting a traditional Afghan flute or pen. The inspiration for this came from the poem "Beshnō een nay" ("Listen to this reed") by the Sufi mystic poet Rumi.

> "Listen to this reed-flute, how it
>   complains,
> It tells stories of separation pains.
> Since they cut me away from the
>   reed bed,
> Men and women have cried into
>   my head."

Khalvatgar was appointed director of Nai and ran it for three years until 2008. He left briefly to join the Open Society Foundation as a media coordinator before returning to Nai in 2010 as general director of training and advocacy. Under his direction, it became the leading advocacy group for journalists in the country. He was instrumental in starting a research department and establishing a two-year diploma program in journalism.

This was an exciting, stimulating, and creative time for Khalvatgar. Developing Nai was part of a broader vision that saw a free and vital press as one of the essential cornerstones of an emerging, democratic civil society in Afghanistan. He was starting with a clean slate and funding from the United States Agency for International Development, the Norwegian Foreign Ministry, and the Canadian International Development Agency. Soon Nai had 152 employees and a national reach with offices in Herat, Jalalabad, and Kandahar in addition to Kabul. Students were flocking to their diploma program, which was shorter than the journalism degrees offered by the universities and, most importantly, provided the kinds of technical and practical skills that the university programs did not. In time, over one thousand students would graduate with the Nai imprimatur.

It was not all plain sailing, however. The Afghan government, notoriously corrupt, was not particularly partial to a local news organization that was churning out graduates who could ask it awkward questions. But the Afghan government was also deeply beholden to Western donors and had to play by a new set of rules that did not tolerate openly quashing a free press and intimidating journalists. So they resorted to espousing the kind of lofty democratic ideals the donors wanted to hear while working quietly to make life difficult for Nai. It was a classic passive-aggressive response. In repeated fits of pique, the government held up approving journalist credentials for Nai employees and delayed responding to Nai's mandatory twice-yearly filing of reports to the relevant Ministries.

More worrying to Khalvatgar was the deteriorating security situation in Afghanistan. The Taliban may have been soundly defeated but they had not gone away. To tackle the growing insurgency, President Obama despatched another thirty thousand troops to the country in 2009. This was in addition to the seventy thousand troops already authorized. Simultaneously, NATO and other U.S. allies boosted their forces to fifty thousand. Journalists were not immune from the escalating violence. According to statistics kept by the Committee to Protect Journalists, no journalists were killed in the four years that followed the defeat of the Taliban. But this changed in 2006 when three journalists were murdered. The killings continued steadily after that, reaching a peak in 2018 with the deaths of fourteen members of the press. Since 2001, sixty-five journalists, of whom nine were female, have been killed in Afghanistan.

It was inevitable that Nai, and by extension Khalvatgar, would get caught in this web of escalating violence. The organization's high profile in a burgeoning Afghan media and their vision of a free press, untethered from government control and inclusive of women, was the very antithesis of what the Taliban had brutally enforced when they controlled the country. In 2014, Nai began receiving threatening letters accusing it of promoting "Western and Jewish values." When Nai celebrated World Press Freedom Day on May 3, 2016, threatening telephone calls were received. The organization was expressly warned that it would not be allowed to follow "Western values and culture." Khalvatgar reported the threats to the office of the second vice president, Sarwar Danish, who was responsible for dealing with security matters involving the government and the institutions of civil society. He was told vaguely that the threats emanated from Southern Afghanistan, where the Taliban were known to have support.

The dangers for Khalvatgar intensified after an interview he gave to the BBC in 2017 in which he called on the Afghan government to stop recruitment broadcasts from a mobile Taliban radio station. A few days later, the radio station was bombed by the Americans and a number of Taliban killed. Khalvatgar never knew whether the bombing was a coincidence, coming so soon after his interview, or premeditated because of his interview. In terms of his personal safety, the distinction was moot because the Taliban blamed him for what had occurred. The group posted a message on their website and on their Facebook page saying he should be killed.

In response, the government offered Khalvatgar an armored car and body guards. He refused. He believed measures like these would separate him from ordinary Afghans. What he did request, however, was that the government pass on any specific threats against him and Nai detected by their intelligence services. They agreed to this and so began a deadly cat-and-mouse scenario as Khalvatgar tried to stay one step ahead of his assassins. He changed his route to and from the office. He regularly switched cars. He varied the times he traveled back and forth to work. He installed an array of security cameras in his home covering every entry point, the periphery, and surrounding walkways from multiple angles. I recall feeling aghast at the level of scrutiny that Khalvatgar and his family had to endure after he gave me a virtual Skype tour of his home and I saw the bank of computer screens displaying grainy live images of his domicile.

By now, the heady optimism that followed in the wake of the Taliban route after 9/11 had dissipated. The fundamentalists continued gaining ground, claiming battlefield successes against a demoralized Afghan army that remained reliant on the American military to bail them out. In the cities, suicide bombings and targeted assassinations were increasing. For Afghans, a terrible history was repeating itself. After a brief respite, it was the age of terror once again.

In 2016, the acclaimed Afghan photographer Shah Marai wrote a blog for his employer, Agence France Presse. It was a cry from the heart by a brave man. "... there is no more hope ... I don't dare to take my children for a walk. I have five and they spend their time cooped up inside the house. Every morning as I go to the office and every evening when I return home, all I think of are cars that can be booby-trapped, or of suicide bombers coming out of a crowd. I can't take the risk. So we don't go out ... I have never felt life to have so little prospects and I don't see a way out."

Marai's words were prophetic. On Monday, April 30, 2018, the Taliban killed him in a double-suicide bombing that also took the lives of eight other journalists. This was the environment in which Khalvatgar and his colleagues were now working. To be sure, life had become hazardous for all Afghans, but journalists and news agencies were a favored Taliban target. The insurgents may have had a fundamentalist, Dark Ages mindset, but they were media savvy. Bludgeon the press, kill the messenger, and control the narrative. Khalvatgar knew this all too well. Given his precarious personal situation, he could have left Afghanistan and joined a brother and sister who were by now well settled in the United States. Relatives, including his mother, were urging him to leave.

But he chose to stay. He saw the chal-

Khalvatgar with journalism student outside his Nai office, Kabul, Afghanistan.

lenge facing his country as a "competition between light and darkness." "I will stay until there is no more light," he told me. His motivation came from the values he believed in: freedom of expression, the right of people to speak freely, to be informed about what was going on in their country. He still held to the dream that had taken flight when Nai came into being. Too much had been achieved to let it all slip away. Afghan civil society, battered as it was by the Taliban, desperately needed a free press. Leaving now would be an act of omission, a source of personal regret and guilt.

To stand firm in the face of terror took great physical courage on Khalvatgar's part. But his choice of language in explaining why he would not walk away points to something deeper. This was a struggle of "light versus darkness" and "rights versus wrongs" and to endure required a moral courage. It was not enough to sprout the importance of a free press—one had to provide the building blocks to make this happen. Listening to Khalvatgar frame his motivation in these terms reminded me

of what a young Bob Dylan had to say in a 1964 *New Yorker* interview: "It's like when somebody wants to tell me what the 'moral' thing is to do. I want them to *show* me. If they have anything to say about morals, I want to know what it is they *do.*"

Khalvatgar continued to "*do*" what he could for a free Afghanistan, driven in part by a moral imperative, until he could do no more. He was at his desk in his Nai office on the morning of August 15, 2021, when the Taliban entered Kabul. His brother phoned and told him not to return home. The Taliban had already come looking for him. The Canadian and French governments, alarmed for his safety, were offering a safe haven. Faced with either being killed, the most likely outcome, or rendered voiceless by the Taliban, he chose exile. The light that he had looked to, which kept him defiantly tethered to his country, had finally been extinguished. It took another three fraught days and nights and repeatedly braving the heaving, desperate crowds ringing Kabul International Airport with the risk of detection by the Taliban, for

Khalvatgar and his immediate family to make it through to a Canadian military transport plane. In the frantic melee at the airport gates, his frail mother was separated from him and missed the flight.

As the giant CC-177 Globemaster lifted off from the runway and his tormented, traumatized country fell away from him, Khalvatgar's first emotion was one of enormous relief. One year later, on the first anniversary of the fall of the Afghan government, safely ensconced in stable, safe, and generous Canada, he has found meaningful work helping the children of Afghan refugees settle into the Canadian school system. His own children are integrating into a new way of life. Many daunting challenges lie ahead, but their collective future, viewed through a Canadian lens, offers hope and stability.

The same sadly cannot be said for the country they left behind. The Taliban, as predicted, has decimated Afghan media. Women are again repressed. Nai is a rump of its former self, the research and advocacy divisions closed, a few support staff remaining, its leadership in exile. Twenty years of Khalvatgar's professional labors have come to naught, blown away by intolerance and revanchism. That he held true to his moral compass is a source of comfort to him. "I feel proud and happy that I could serve my country for two decades," he told me.

But then again, we are talking about Afghanistan, the Graveyard of Empires, a land where any coda at best must end on a note of pathos. Abdul Mujeeb Khalvatgar labored passionately in a good cause. When that was upended, and staying put likely meant a violent death, he was able to steer himself, his wife, and children—but not his mother—to safe waters. When you meet the man, he exudes calmness and a quiet confidence. But behind this façade, other emotions lurk. "I feel lost, absent," he once divulged to me. And in these few poignant words, we surely glimpse what millions of his fellow Afghans must be feeling too.

Larysa Shchyrakova. Gomel, Belarus.

Larysa Shchyrakova

Pause for a moment and reflect on the following situation playing out as you read these words. A forty-eight-year-old single mother keeps a small suitcase packed and constantly at the ready. It contains a few basic toiletries and change of clothes. She will need it when the KGB agents knock on her door and she is taken off to prison. She has one child, a fifteen-year-old son. The boy has two grandparents. They are aware of their daughter's precarious situation. They fear for her. When the time comes, they will do what they can for their grandson, but they are elderly.

This family trauma is a throwback to Stalinist times, but Stalin has been dead for sixty-eight years and the Soviet empire he spawned crumbled thirty years back. The winds of change may have blown across the Ural Mountains, up through the Baltics and swept the Russian steppes, but they have done so unevenly—and when it comes to Belarus, they have petered out. The woman with the packed valise is journalist Larysa Shchyrakova. This is how she lives under the dictatorship of Belarus President Alexander Lukashenko.

The plight of Belarusian journalists was dramatically illustrated on May 23, 2021, when a Ryanair flight from Athens to Vilnius traveling over Belarusian airspace was forced to land in the capital, Minsk, because of a bogus bomb scare. On board was Roman Protasevich, a twenty-six-year-old Belarusian journalist living in exile in Lithuania, whose reportage critical of the Lukashenko regime had angered the dictator. Protasevich and his girlfriend, Sofia Sapega, were removed from the plane by Belarusian security forces and he soon

Above: *Working from home.*

From the very beginning of her career, Shchyrakova saw journalism as a way of helping her fellow citizens by keeping them informed of events within their repressed country.

appeared on state television offering a mea culpa. Seen alongside this flagrant act of air piracy and kidnapping, it is understandable why Shchyrakova has her overnight bag packed.

Larysa Shchyrakova is not a journalist by training. She studied history at Francisk Skorina Gomel State University, focusing on Belarusian history between the two World Wars. After graduating, she began working as a secondary school teacher. She was in her mid-thirties, divorced and raising her then three-year-old son, when a friend asked her if she would like to join Belsat TV, the only independent Belarusian TV station. With headquarters in Warsaw, the company's mission statement is to give Belarusians access to independent news on the situation in their country. When Belsat was founded in 2007, Lukashenko was one year into his third term and his rule was becoming increasingly dictatorial. He reportedly referred to the new station as "stupid and uncongenial," and his administration refused to register it as a foreign news agency.

Bored with her work as a teacher, Shchyrakova took up her friend's offer and switched careers. Unlike her previous job, there was no fixed, unchanging curriculum that she had to follow year after year. Now there were new stories every day, something different to engage her attention. From the very beginning of her career, she saw journalism as a way of helping her fellow citizens by keeping them informed of events within their country. To do so, she was given a broad portfolio to cover that included politics, corruption, culture, and social affairs.

At the time, government repression in Belarus was not as extreme as it is today, but democracy was already under siege. Lukashenko would go on to claim victory in three more elections in 2010, 2015, and 2020—the last of which was marred by widespread election fraud, the brutal suppression of mass protests, and the forced exile to Lithuania of the country's main opposition leader, Sviatlana Tsikhanouskaya.

With civil liberties progressively eroding, it became clear to Shchyrakova that her fellow citizens were being left completely unprotected by the law. "Sometimes the only hope for them is an article in the paper or a reference to them on television," she said. This realization continues to motivate her work, aligning her journalism with social justice.

As Louis Pasteur observed, fortune favors the prepared mind. Shchyrakova did not arrive at this juncture in her life through happenstance alone. To be sure, the repressive Lukashenko regime created the societal pressures that led to citizens resisting his diktats, but Shchyrakova's activism predates the coming of the Belarusian strongman. When perestroika began in the 1980s, she was a teenager. Suddenly, there was this "wave of information about the terrible Soviet past," she recalled. She could now read Aleksandr Solzhenitsyn openly. It was, as she put it, a "breath of freedom." Despite the hardships induced by an economy that was being forced to change rapidly, resulting in empty supermarket shelves and people queueing in long lines for basic commodities, she remembers this period fondly. "These were fantastic times" she told me.

When she was twenty, Shchyrakova joined Talaka, a youth NGO that promoted the Belarusian language and culture. During the decades of Russian occupation, a nationalistic apartheid of sorts had taken root. Russian became the lingua franca, dominating the cultural and intellectual landscape in Belarus. Only "ignorant peasants from the countryside were thought to speak Belarusian," she told me. Talaka was formed to counteract this cultural imperialism. In an act of defiance, Shchyrakova made a point of speaking Belarusian everywhere, even though the authorities regarded those who did so with suspicion.

A few weeks before I interviewed Shchyrakova, Talaka was "liquidated," to use Shchyrakova's term, joining over forty-five NGOs accused of being a fifth column and shut down by the Lukashenko regime. The absurdity of an organization promoting Belarusian culture being viewed as a threat to the country itself underscores the Kafkaesque logic that underpins Lukashenko's rule.

Shchyrakova struggled at first with

Shchyrakova with her parents. Minsk, Belarus.

Shchyrakova with her son.

aspects of her new career. Certain challenges, such as learning to use cameras, were quickly overcome—whereas others, such as adapting to continual government harassment, have remained perennially taxing. Belsat has repeatedly been denied accreditation by the Lukashenko regime. Without it, the media group is not considered a legal entity—which leaves it, and Shchyrakova, open to prosecution. Since 2016, she has been in court over forty times, fined each time for working without accreditation. In 2017, she was threatened with having her son taken away from her because she was being detained so often.

The emotional blackmail did not end there. The State Security Committee, which is still known as the KGB in Belarus, created a website with the express purpose of exposing the private lives of journalists considered a threat to the state. Shchyrakova's telephone calls have been monitored, her computer hacked, and emails with details of her personal life sent to her parents and neighbors and also made public. Having her private life

exposed in this way has inevitably affected her relationships. She has coped with this by learning to ignore the opinion of others. "If you cannot develop this immunity, you have to leave journalism" is how she sees the challenge.

Some forms of persecution are, however, harder to ignore. Her home has been searched twice recently. The searches happened early in the morning, rousing her and her son from sleep. Since then, she finds herself waking up at the same time every morning anticipating another search, her internal alarm matching the time the KGB came calling. "I am like Pavlov's dog," she said, an insightful reference to her behavioral response conditioned by fear. "I am eternally waiting for arrest."

Her son also has been affected by this harassment. He was five years old when he witnessed the first KGB search of his home, unknown men going through all their possessions. He was fourteen when he saw his mother being arrested for the first time. Witnessing her being detained again last year rekindled earlier anxieties, leaving him hypervigilant. He now checks up on her whereabouts, needing to know where she is. From time to time, Shchyrakova sees him peering out of a window at home, looking for suspicious cars—a throwback to the "Black Marias," evocative slang for the vehicles used by the secret police to cart off Soviet citizens to jail (or worse) during Stalin's Great Terror.

The factors motivating Shchyrakova to continue her work, despite the harassment and toll it has taken on her and her family, are both principled and practical. At her age, the prospect of fleeing Belarus with her son, leaving behind her family and friends, and being forced to live with meager financial resources in a cheap rental or refugee shelter, is anathema. "What would I do career-wise, then, if journalism was not possible?" she asks herself. "Cleaner? Sales person?" Furthermore, she sees her work as a "moral obligation." The independent media in Belarus has been blocked. Many journalists have fled the country, and according to the Committee to Protect Journalists, at least ten are currently behind bars. "I have to stay," she insisted. "I have to withstand the pressure."

This ethical imperative goes to the very heart of her moral courage. Rushworth Kidder, founder of the Institute for Global Ethics, which studies shared moral values and how institutions and individuals can put them into practice, has identified three core components to moral courage: principles, endurance, and danger. Shchyrakova ticks all three boxes. From the moment she joined Belsat, she has worked tirelessly to uphold one of the key foundations of a democratic society—namely, a free press. She has pursued this moral imperative for twelve dangerous years, during which the state, wielding its vast powers, has tried to intimidate her into submission. To endure, she has tapped into this wellspring of moral courage by framing her struggle in terms of the values it represents.

"I am an honest person. Those who arrest me are the criminals. There are many respectable people in prison now, and I will be one of them," she asserted. "I am working for a better future—to lead a normal

One of Shchyrakova's cameras seized by the police.

life and not to be afraid of the police, of persecution; to live in a normal democracy and be protected by the law." It is a rationale she has used as well with her mother, who has tried repeatedly to dissuade her daughter from journalism, imploring her to return to her work as a teacher, a safer bet in a police state.

Maternal disapproval of her work is yet one more stressor Shchyrakova copes with. She loves her mother, but views her as timid—attributing this lifelong trait to the circumstances of her mother's birth on Christmas Eve during the Second World War, in a house occupied by soldiers from Hitler's Wehrmacht. While impossible to prove or refute, her theory does call to mind James Baldwin's observation that people are trapped in history and history is trapped in them—an axiom perhaps underscored by the fate of Shchyrakova's maternal great-grandfather. Rygor Kavalchuk was forty years old when he was arrested in the late 1930s and never seen again. She believes he likely criticized the folly of collective farms, an opinion that

was enough to sign a person's death warrant in those times. In 2019, Shchyrakova started a campaign called "Killed and Forgotten" to remember and honor the many Belarusians killed by Stalin's regime.

The gulags may be gone now, but the Lukashenko regime has not entirely discarded Koba's playbook. Seventy years after Rygor Kavalchuck's disappearance, his great-granddaughter awaits her knock on the door—history redux. Her young son anxiously waits with her. To prepare him for the moment, she has told him that she has committed no crime, even though she knows truth offers them no protection. She has asked him not to become depressed by her anticipated arrest, to remain calm and send her daily letters of support when she is in prison. And she tries to reassure him that she will come back to him—in a year or less, she surmises—and everything will ultimately be okay.

Her boy responds with disbelief and bemusement—with the innocence of youth, he cannot comprehend how a good person can be jailed for doing nothing wrong.

Mosaed in exile. Washington, DC, USA.

Mohammad Mosaed

"When you are born in a country like Iran, you can never be free."

This is how journalist Mohammad Mosaed described his current plight to me. After his prolonged ordeal at the hands of the Iranian government culminating in his desperate flight into exile, I could readily understand his grim, fatalistic outlook. Listening to his life story, however, also made me think of another explanation that could account for the path his life had taken—one that did not negate his view, but rather offered a complementary understanding of how he came to find himself in Washington DC, looking over his shoulder, anticipating fresh threats.

"Until you make the unconscious conscious," wrote Carl Gustav Jung, "it will direct your life and you will call it fate."

To put Jung's theory to the test, we need to take a closer look at Mosaed's early years. He was born during a great upheaval. The Manjil–Rudbar earthquake had struck northern Iran, devastating the area and forcing his mother to travel from Sowme'eh Sara, her hometown, to Gorgan, in the state of Golestan, to give birth to him. When young Mohammad was six years of age, his father, a teacher, obtained a post in the village of Abatar, closer to the city they had left to escape the earthquake's devastation.

The school only had two classrooms. One was used to teach students. The other was home to the Mosaed family, which by now included a second son. Despite his father being a teacher, Mosaed's family was impoverished. Power to their single-room dwelling was supplied by a battery. In northern Iran, the sun sets early in winter.

Above: The shoes that Mosaed was wearing when he escaped from Iran to Turkey, walking across the Zagros mountains in winter and almost freezing to death.

[57]

If the family wanted electric light, there would be no hot water. If hot water was needed, the light came from a candle.

These were the kind of decisions Mosaed recalls his parents having to make daily. And while there was always something to eat, it was not unusual to have only one meal a day. The family lived this way for four years, and tough as it was, Mosaed regarded himself as fortunate. He was aware, even at that tender age, of others having it worse.

Ten years after the earthquake that had killed an estimated forty-two thousand people, Mosaed's family moved back to Sowme'eh Sara. He was enrolled in a school for gifted children from poor families. From there, he gained entry to the University of Rasht, where he studied computer science and worked as a mechanic to support himself. While at university, he continued something he had been doing since elementary school: writing stories. At first, he wrote fiction. Some of his published work came to the attention of an editor at *Chelcheragh*, a popular weekly magazine

with a young readership. He was a offered a part-time job covering local news in the north of Iran.

Mosaed's nascent career as a journalist was interrupted by compulsory national service. He recalls two difficult years housed in a police station, working long hours seven days a week without pay, living off lousy food and being forbidden to write. No sooner was this ordeal behind him than he began working full time for *Shargh*, a reformist newspaper. Tasked with writing about the economy, he gravitated toward exposing corruption—fertile yet dangerous grounds for an investigative reporter in Iran.

Iranian journalists are understandably hesitant to write about corruption in their country. Ranked 172nd out of 180 nations by Reporters Without Borders when it comes to an index of press freedom, Iran deals harshly with journalists who expose inconvenient truths. Intimidation, arrests, beatings, torture, targeting family members—there's a playbook of cruelty designed to muzzle an independent press.

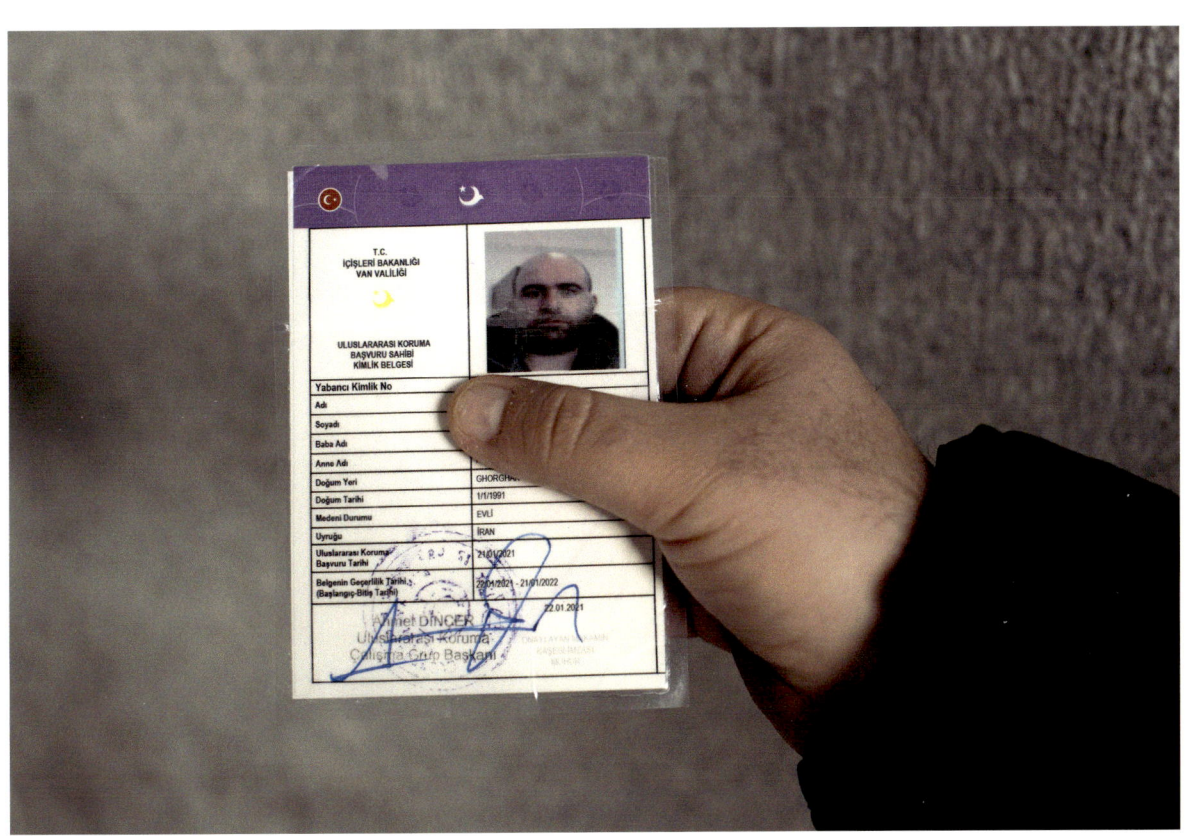

Mosaed's Turkish identity document given to him after he fled Iran.

Now in exile, the journalist reflects on his long and arduous road from Abatar, Iran.

Mosaed would have known this before he began asking his questions. Still, he never hesitated. He was not alone in seeing corruption as a major cause of Iran's poverty, wealth disparity, delayed development, and social crises. He was, however, one of the very few within Iran to shine a light on it.

One of the approaches the Iranian government uses to deal with corruption has been the establishment of anticorruption courts. What Mosaed revealed was that these courts are corrupt as well, thus perpetuating the problem. The regime's response to his exposé was to ban him from entering the court building. His editor at *Sharg* also told him to leave the anticorruption courts alone. It was simply too dangerous to continue.

Mosaed's response was to shift his attention to the government's corrupt practice of selling off state companies to the private sector, a process rife with nepotism, bribery, kickbacks, and skimming. In the process, workers lost their jobs and livelihoods, and when they protested, they were arrested. This kind of reporting was too

risky for *Sharg*, as well. The paper received calls from the government to warn him off. "I would hand in a four-thousand-word article, and only two thousand words would be printed. Some of my reports were suppressed completely," Mosaed told me. He recalls his editor pleading with him: "It's not a free country, be careful." For three years, the paper walked a tight-rope, keen to keep him because of his big readership while simultaneously trying to placate the regime.

Mosaed chaffed at this in-house censorship. Worse still, when national protests erupted over the state of the economy and the falling value of the rial, a cowed *Sharg*, like other mainstream media in the country, remained completely silent. Mosaed could contain his anger no longer. He turned to Twitter to write about things his paper would not print.

"I used the backdoor to avoid the censor," he told me. Almost overnight, he found a huge audience, ten times *Sharg*'s circulation. The government, with its antennae finely tuned to the influential sway of online material, tried to still his criticism by pressuring *Sharg* to shut his Twitter account. Mosaed refused to back off, threatening to resign if the paper forced him to cut off his Twitter feed.

In November 2019, he was arrested. The circumstances of how he was taken into custody were choreographed to traumatize not only him, but his family, too. He had gone to spend a few days at his parents' house. One morning, he awoke to find a stranger in his bedroom filming him with a camcorder. The man was a security agent of the IRGC, the Islamic Revolutionary Guard Corps. He was accompanied by two fellow agents, one of whom was female and brought along to restrain Mosaed's mother should the need arise.

This fealty to religious sensibilities brings to mind Blaise Pascal's trenchant observation that men never do evil so completely and cheerfully as when they do it from religious conviction. Mosaed watched the agents go through clothing and books, looking for incriminating evidence in the absence of a crime. His hands were tied behind his back. The last thing he saw before being blindfolded was his horrified father shouting in protest and being manhandled aside as he tried to come to his assistance.

Three weeks of solitary confinement in an IRGC cell followed. The tiny two-by-three-meter room had no window or bed. The light was kept on constantly. A camera monitored Mosaed's every moment. He was not allowed access to a lawyer. He could not see his family. He would be taken, blindfolded, at all hours to an interrogation room where he was questioned by two men "playing good cop, bad cop," as he described it to me. And he was tortured. These were terrifying days for him. "They government did not want facts," he recalls. "They wanted repentance and to leave me as a broken person with no courage to challenge them."

Mosaed never buckled. He was released on bail after three weeks, with his parents' house as surety. He was ordered to stay off social media, but no sooner was he released than he reopened his Twitter account. The state responded by arresting his fiancé, Ashraf Nafari, keeping her in Qarchak prison for two weeks before transferring her to the notorious Evin prison for another three months. Only then did he stop writing.

When Mosaed finally appeared in the revolutionary court, he was given a token lawyer. His case was heard by Iman Afshari, a mullah who was in a hurry and asked a few perfunctory questions before telling Mosaed to go home and await his sentence. The court proceedings lasted less than fifteen minutes. Two days later, he was sentenced to four years and nine months in jail, followed by a two-year ban on working as a journalist in addition to a further three months of mandatory work for the government as a social worker.

Mosaed was spared serving his harsh sentence by the cumbersome cogs of a totalitarian bureaucracy. It might take only a few minutes to condemn an innocent man to years in jail, but the paperwork that opens the gates to Evin prison cannot be rushed. In the weeks it took to process the mullah's decision, Mosaed, out on bail, fled to Turkey. His hurried farewell to his parents was harrowing.

After taking a train to Khoy, close to the Turkish border, he set out to cross the snowy Zagros mountains in winter at night. Human traffickers involved in the organ trade were active in the area, adding to his anxiety. Despite a full moon lighting the way, he got lost and almost froze to death. In desperation, his clothes frozen stiff, he called 911 and reached Turkish emergency services. At first, the Turkish authorities wanted to deport him back to Iran, but interventions from the Committee to Protect Journalists among other organizations aware of his plight, secured his freedom.

Nafari joined him in Ankara and the couple hunkered down for five months, fearful of venturing outdoors lest they be assassinated or kidnapped by Iranian agents. This fear has lessened but not abated with their move to Washington. Mosaed still sleeps poorly. He struggles daily with painful memories. One begins to appreciate the depths of his despair when

محمد مساعد
@mohammadmosaed

Knock knock! Hello Free World!
I used 42 different proxy to write
this! Millions of Iranians don't have
internet. Can you hear us?

#Internet4Iran

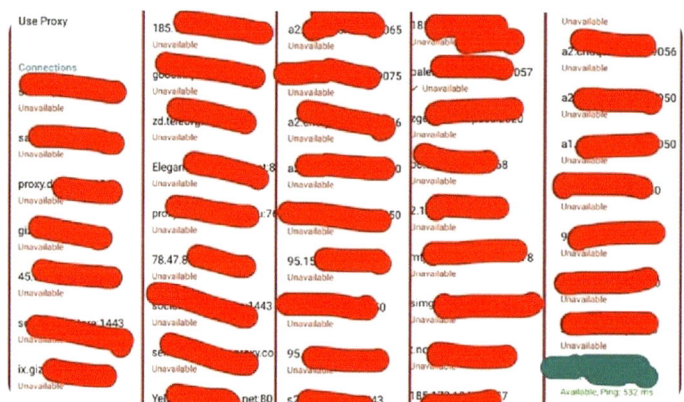

3:34 AM · 19 Nov 19 · Twitter for Android

3,104 Retweets   **6,882** Likes

Mosaed's Twitter message.

he candidly admits he does not have the "energy and courage" to continue with his psychotherapy.

As for Mosaed's parents, they are trying to hold on to their house, which the Iranian regime has laid claim to as forfeiture for their son's flight while on bail. That his parents have been placed in this predicament weighs heavily on him, too. He has told them to disown him, hoping this might save their home. All of which explains his cri-de-coeur that, as an Iranian, he will never be free.

Mosaed comes across as quietly spoken, thoughtful, and exceedingly polite. I cannot claim to know him well after one interview, but I would be surprised if proved wrong in also viewing him as eminently gentle, patient, and kind. But beneath the mild demeanor is a remarkable moral courage that has driven and sustained him in his darkest hours.

In order to understand where his moral code comes from, let us return to Jung and his view of how the unconscious influences behavior. Mosaed did not chose to write about corruption in Iran by chance. What steered him in this direction were remote childhood experiences, some remembered, others not, all infused with emotions he would not have understood or even been aware of at the time. The indignity of poverty marked the child, and in doing so forged the man he would become.

Corruption on a grand scale that impoverished millions of citizens, that forced a school teacher and his family to live out of a classroom without privacy or basic amenities, even as billions of petrodollars gushed into state coffers, is a moral outrage. As a child, Mosaed lacked the intellectual capacity to see it as such, but he smelled and tasted poverty during his formative years and the visceral memory of it never left him.

Grinding poverty can hold generations captive. Mosaed, in breaking free, sees himself as having been given a "lucky chance" to bring about change. As he explained it to me: "It is my responsibility to my past, my family, my community." It is a theme he returned to repeatedly—this moral imperative to expose corruption for the greater good. "It is not just about me, it is about millions of people."

Refusing to stay silent has come at considerable personal cost to Mosaed: torture, exile, the imprisonment of his fiancée, a deep loneliness from a life without friends (too dangerous for them, too risky for him, the paranoia of fear cutting both ways), remorse propelling his request to be disowned. Each of these morally egregious situations has been foisted on him by a vengeful regime, and they all could have been avoided by staying quiet.

When I put this to Mosaed, he dismissed my assumption out of hand. Doing nothing, he asserted, would be worse than all he has endured. Presented this way, we can see the degree to which moral injury, and its foil, moral courage, have determined his behavior. Remaining silent, an act of omission, has never been an option, for it opens the door to the shame that follows in moral injury's wake. "They cannot silence me," he asserted. "If we cannot talk about the problem, how can we solve it?" Expanding on this further, he believes "the worst thing is to say what the government wants." To do so means the regime "has broken you. After that you breathe and eat and sleep, but can do nothing more."

The road from Abatar to Washington has been long and arduous for Mosaed. What comes next will not be easy for him and his fiancée. But as he navigates an uncertain future, there is one certainty that he can hold on to, and it will surely comfort him: He remained true to his moral compass.

In doing so, he touched the lives of countless Iranians who avidly read his columns each week, who followed him on Twitter, who learned about things in their country the government wanted hidden, and who would come up to him on the streets of Tehran to offer a quiet thank-you.

Dixit photographed while working on a story of urban poverty. New Delhi, India.

Neha Dixit

India, with a population of 1.4 billion people, of whom 600 million voted in the 2019 general election, considers itself the world's largest democracy. A different set of numbers, however, undercuts this assertion. Since Prime Minister Narendra Modi came to power in 2014, the country has fallen 26 places on the Economist Intelligence Unit's Democracy Index—from 27 to 53. So steep and rapid has been India's democratic decline, Sweden's V-Dem (Varieties of Democracy) Institute no longer considers the country an electoral democracy, but rather an electoral autocracy, a step just above closed autocracies like China, Libya, and Afghanistan.

To understand India's slippery descent, one should read the reportage of Neha Dixit, a thirty-seven-year-old New Delhi–based freelance journalist. Her exposure of the deep strains of racism and misogyny that currently course through Indian society, nurtured by a resurgent militant nationalism that stokes intolerance for political gain, has made life hazardous for her. She could not have anticipated the harassment that over time has engulfed her career, but even if she had, I doubt it would have deflected her from her course. Not with her finely set moral compass.

Dixit grew up in an upper-middle-class family in Lucknow, in the state of Uttar Pradesh, approximately 500 kilometers from New Delhi. Her father worked in a government bank and her mother was a teacher. Education was prized in her family, and although young Neha excelled at school with a 90 percent average, she remembers being pressured to match her brother, whose grades were in the mid 90s.

Above: India has a wide range of journalism available, but little of it supports democratic goals.

An independent, free spirit, which would become evident in her work as a journalist, was present at an early age. Unbeknownst to her parents, and bucking rigid gender-based conventions in Lucknow, she rode a scooter. Neighbors, aghast at her behavior, informed her parents of this and moreover let them know she rode fast and honked at boys.

Looking beyond these adolescent peccadillos, however, were more serious disagreements with her parents. They opposed her desire to become a journalist. Her father was influenced by his father, who saw the profession as little more than stenography, a clerical position, not suited for a woman. Studying in New Delhi was also frowned upon, the city viewed as a gateway to drinking, smoking, and falling pregnant. Rather stay put, they urged her, and study medicine.

Dixit would have none of it. She did not want to be a doctor. Rote learning was not for her. She liked writing and poetry and already, by thirteen years of age, had had some of her work published in a community paper. She was determined to go her own way, to escape what she saw as the "crystalized choice of her parents."

"You have aged me by ten years." This rebuke from Dixit's father as she set about her studies in New Delhi came to haunt her. Within six years of her leaving home, he was dead. While the cause of death was complications arising from diabetes, Dixit has never fully shaken off the guilt she felt at his passing.

Misplaced guilt aside, university proved liberating. As Dixit recalls, a liberal milieu at Miranda House, a college for women at the University of Delhi, afforded her a "chance to understand the world." Her newfound freedoms away from the rigid conformities of life in Lucknow offered small, unexpected pleasures, as well. She could wear her hair loose without fear of being judged amoral and being stalked. To her amazement, she could even go to a midnight movie on her own. Shedding the constraints of a controlling patriarchy allowed her to see that her relationship with her father was indicative of what

Dixit photographed at her residence.

Dixit, at home, sifts through old editions of magazines that have published her news stories. She has maintained a collection of hard copies of magazines that have published her work over the course of her career.

women in India endured. Insights like this steered her toward women's rights issues. It was part of her awakening as a woman in a tolerant university environment, and it set her career course.

By the time she was twenty-two years of age, Dixit had completed an undergraduate degree majoring in English and a two-year master's degree in journalism, the latter from AJK Mass Communication Centre, a constituent institute of the Jamia Millia Islamia, also in New Delhi. To forestall family pressure to return home and settle into the conformity of an arranged marriage, she never told her parents that her studies were complete or that she had subsequently taken a stopgap position for a tech company writing content. A month later, she landed her first journalism position writing for *Tehelka*, a news magazine known for investigative journalism and sting operations.

Her first cover story reported on human trafficking in India and the sexual exploitation that accompanied it. Women were being sold off as brides. Her research took her into red light districts, which appalled her father. He beseeched her not to share this story with family members. Good girls stayed away from such areas, he admonished her.

Another of her stories exposed the honor killing of women. Diktats from courts in northern India held that women could not choose their partners. Those who did ran the risk of being killed. Moreover, there was no accountability for the extrajudicial killings.

Stories like these infuriated conservative, reactionary elements within Indian society. Social media had yet to take off, but blogs were popular and one way to threaten a journalist. Dixit was warned that she would be beaten "black and blue." She recalls being chased away from more remote mining areas where she had gone to collect firsthand accounts of gender-based violence. The pressures and dangers that came her way were endured alone. No support was offered. The responses from management at *Tehelka* were either to compliment her on her bravery or to normalize the experience as just one of those things that came with this type of work.

Looking back on this nascent period in her career, Dixit recalls that her toughest challenge was not the incipient violence that dogged her steps, but rather the sexual harassment she had to endure from her editor. At the time, there was simply no recourse for her to deal with it. This was not only a *Tehelka*-related problem, she realized, but a systemic issue faced by women journalists elsewhere. And unhappy as she was about it, she could not simply up and leave her hard-won position, because, as she saw it, doing so would prove her family right and all the pressures for her to return home and be married off would crank up again. "It was very difficult not having any moral support," she divulged. "I was quite alone and very young."

Despite the pressures that came with her work, Dixit liked what she was doing. She pushed back against the constant urgings of her family to pursue film journalism, a safer and less controversial career path than the one she had set her sights on. Bolstering her resolve was the impact her stories were having, like her exposé of child labor practices that led to the rescue of 250 children. An outcome like this validated her work and kept her motivated to pursue socially relevant, albeit emotionally fraught, issues.

After three years at *Tehelka*, Dixit wanted to try television journalism and took a position on the investigative desk at *India Today*. Her switch to TV pleased her family. Not only could they now see her on the air, but they could also use her screen presence to attract potential suitors for an arranged marriage by telling them to "check her out." What they would have seen during Dixit's thirty minutes on the air was a journalist committed to exposing morally egregious behavior perpetrated by people with power. Her topics ranged from honor killings to the use of child soldiers by Maoist insurgents (fighting the Indian government in remote rural areas for better land rights and jobs), to the dubious ethical practices of Big Pharma. In relation to the latter, she revealed how pharmaceutical companies were undertaking clinical trials on poor, abandoned mentally ill patients in government hospitals in the state of Madhya Pradesh. Exploiting the most vulnerable of individuals made a mockery of the sacrosanct medical process of informed consent, and patients were paying with their lives and side effects. Her story galvanised the Indian Medical Association into taking action. All clinical trials throughout India were halted for two and a half years to clean shop.

Dixit did not, however, enjoy working in television. She found the medium "very shallow." When a large corporate house bought a 37 percent stake in *India Today* and pushed for stories on the urban mon-eyed class—"rich kids racing fast cars in Delhi"—rather than what were dismissively referred to as "back of the beyond bleeding heart stories," her days in front of the camera were numbered. Two years after joining the station, she resigned and began freelancing, to the bemusement of her family.

Her first freelance story was how Rash-triya Swayamsevak Sangh, a right-wing Hindu nationalist paramilitary organization to which the Bharatiya Janata Party (BJP) of Narendra Modi is closely aligned, was running training camps for young girls in political Hinduism with a militantly racist agenda. She was fortunate to escape unhurt when her cover as a journalist was blown after she had gained entry to one of these camps.

Her next exposé was in late 2013, just before the BJP came to power, when she wrote about a huge sectarian riot in northern India in which over one hundred thousand Muslim people were displaced. The police and local Hindu population were complicit in the communal violence, which included mass rapes and the burning of villages. Dixit had reported on sexual violence before, but the difference this time was that it was confined to Muslim women. Hindu ultranationalists were enraged, and the online trolling and harassment began. She would receive up to three hundred threatening messages a day. Over the years, it has not let up. Her face has been photoshopped onto the bodies of naked women.

Awards won by Dixit for her investigative reporting displayed on a shelf in her home office. She has won a number of prestigious awards over the years including the 2011 Kurk Schork award for International Journalism and the 2019 International Press Freedom Award from the Committee to Protect Journalists (CPJ).

She has been threatened with rape by steel rod or thorny bush. She told me that it has taken her eight or nine years to become numb to the content of these messages.

Disconcerting as the online harassment has been, Dixit is now more worried about two different threats. Three criminal cases have been filed against her over the past six years by Hindu fundamentalists and the Indian state. One of these charges, under section 153A of India's colonial-era penal code, which has been used to silence journalists in the past, concerns "inciting communal hatred through writing." It carries a potential five-year prison term and requires her attendance every two months in the Gauhati High Court, 2000 kilometers away from her home in New Delhi. Here she sits and waits in the accused box at the back of the court room for the judge to renew her bail. This could take a few minutes or a whole day. Failure to attend would trigger an arrest warrant. The process, which has been going on for years, is yet another form of harassment designed to silence her. And the ramifications do not stop here. Many news outlets have stopped publishing her stories, fearing a potentially ruinous, never-ending legal imbroglio by association.

A second major concern is the physical safety of her mother. After she wrote about extrajudicial police killings in her hometown of Lucknow, she received a phone call from a senior local policeman. "We know your mother lives here" was his chilling message. These fears are augmented by worries over her own safety and that of her partner, the documentary maker Nakul Singh Sawhney, who has also received death threats. In 2021, Dixit was stalked for five months. That same year, after being warned online that acid would be thrown in her face, her apartment was broken into. Police took no action to find the culprits.

There has been no letup in Dixit's harassment, even after she stepped away from reporting into academia two years back to write a book. The online abuse continues unabated. She is now damned by reputation. The hate has become self-generating.

When a country touts itself as the world's largest democracy, yet occupies a lowly place—150 out of 180 countries—on a global index of press freedom put out annually by Reporters Without Borders, the contradiction is jarring. Something is rotten in the state of India, and what Dixit has had to endure in her fifteen-year career as a journalist underscores this. But her travails indicate something else as well, a world above yet tethered to, the malign forces that would bring her down. I refer to her remarkable temperament. In the face of relentless, intense harassment, she has not buckled, standing firm on the moral high ground.

She has been able to hold true to her course for complex reasons, not all immediately apparent to her. To be sure, the impact of her reportage has been validating, something the twenty-two-year-old neophyte was keenly aware of. But as she has matured and grown as a person, and the range of her subject matter has broadened with her increasing awareness of the escalating intolerance and demonization of the "other" that has defined the rule of the BJP, a profoundly influential factor has come to the fore in explaining her motivation. There is now a moral imperative that guides her journalism. It is writ large in how she views India today. "It is a democracy only for the rich upper-class Hindu people," she told me. "I feel totally ashamed that this is what we have come to. I did not grow up in a country like this."

Shame in response to morally egregious behaviours—acts of commission—is one part of the moral injury equation. A second part relates to how she should respond to these events. "If I, with all my privileges of caste and religion in this country, don't speak up, who will?" she asks defiantly. Silence is not an option for her, as her journalism reveals, and in speaking up, she avoids the burden of further shame and guilt that comes with an act of omission. Most editors, on the other hand, appear guided by a different moral compass. "They do not want to be on the wrong side of the government," she notes ruefully. "They are spineless, toothless, and only speak up for someone who is really, really famous."

Dixit's momentos, including photographs of family, are displayed beneath a framed wall hanging that reads "Life is beautiful."

Moral courage as the antidote to moral injury comes with a steep price, as Dixit's history reveals. For the past three years, she has been seeing a psychotherapist. She finds the process helpful. But there is one symptom that has proved intractable: nightmares haunt her sleep. The content is always violent, traumatic. She is being stabbed or shot. In one recurring dream, she is walking along the beach as breaking waves fling "shit" at her. One does not need a degree in psychiatry to appreciate the painful symbolism here.

Dixit comes across as an upbeat, lively person, eloquent and passionate in her opinions. But her dreams, the window to her unconscious, reveal a different set of emotions, darker and more ominous. In light of what she has endured, this is not surprising, and it meshes with her outlook for India in at least one respect. "I am not by nature a pessimist," she confided, "but on the gender issue, I am losing hope. Equal rights for women might not happen in my lifetime because we are constantly moving backwards."

Amid this bleak landscape, there are a few residual positives and perhaps some tentative signs of progress. Dixit loves the vibrant culture and diversity of India. She rejects her brother's advice to emigrate. She still believes journalism empowers her, notwithstanding the harassment that comes with it. She has been honored with a number of awards, including the 2014 Kurt Schork Award in International Journalism and the 2019 International Press Freedom Award from the Committee to Protect Journalists (CPJ). Closer to home, two of her female cousins have become journalists, covering film. But most importantly of all, as Dixit sees it, women from many different walks of life have rallied to her side. They, and not media organizations, are her biggest source of support. "They have my back," she told me.

Frenkel editing photographs on his laptop at his home. St. Petersburg, Russia.

David Frenkel

In the summer of 2020, a referendum was held in Russia to amend the country's constitution. On the ballot were changes that allowed President Vladimir Putin to run for two further six-year presidential terms, banned same-sex marriages, enshrined patriotic education in school curricula, and placed the constitution above international law. On June 30, Russian photojournalist David Frenkel received an alert via the messaging app Telegram of potential voting irregularities at a nearby polling station in central St. Petersburg. He hurried over to see what was happening. From what he could discern, the tensions related to the stuffing of a ballot box with fake votes and illegal attempts to remove election officials who were questioning the validity of these votes. Frenkel's sudden appearance in the midst of this commotion was not welcomed by the police and others at the scene he surmised were agent provocateurs.

What transpired next is captured in a brief, disturbing video clip. Frenkel is seen filming the scene on his mobile phone. A police officer, later identified as Sergeant Denis Dmitriyev, approaches him, pushes him backward, and wrestles him to the floor. As he does so, there is an audible crack. Frenkel yells out in pain. The crack is the sound of his arm breaking. As Frenkel lies on the ground in agony, another man subsequently identified as Dmitry Abramov, a former city lawmaker from the ruling United Russia Party, approaches him, accuses him of feigning distress, and yanks on his broken limb. When Frenkel screams in pain, Abramov laughs and walks away.

Frenkel was taken by ambulance to the

Above: *Frenkel photographing citizens protesting to preserve a historic building.*

Frenkel photographing Russian citizens protesting the pending destruction of a historic building.

hospital, where he underwent surgery later that day. Weeks of rehabilitation followed. Ever motivated, he continued his investigative work despite being partly incapacitated following surgery, with his right arm heavily strapped and unable to hold a camera. Along with other colleagues, he worked to shed light on government attempts to block media access to the internet, the administration's manipulation of COVID-19 data to obscure an inept response to the pandemic, and the gross suppression of human rights in Belarus. While Frenkel's assault was widely reported, neither Sergeant Dmitriyev nor Abramov faced disciplinary action. Instead, Frenkel was fined 500 rubles (around 7 US dollars) for failing to obey the officer's instructions.

What is unusual about this episode is not the roughing up of a Russian journalist. After all, when seen alongside the near-fatal Novichok poisoning and subsequent incarceration of opposition leader Alexey Navalny, a fractured arm is essentially small print in terms of state sanctioned human rights abuses. Rather, what stands out in this sorry episode is that twenty-nine-year-old Frenkel is a physicist with a degree from ITMO University, one of Russia's leading higher education and research institutions. His particular expertise is in liquid crystals.

That Frenkel came to find himself with a camera recording voting irregularities may be traced in large measure to his outrage at President Putin's increasingly dictatorial rule and the unraveling of the rule of law in Russia today. "For some people in Russia, it has become uncomfortable just to do your job," he explained. "Being a scientist, it's not enough. You do your job, you do it well, but it's not enough to be a good person anymore." For those Russians like Frenkel, who view the unraveling of a nascent democracy hard won following the years of perestroika and glasnost as unacceptable, silence is not an option. Passivity is intolerable. Saying and doing nothing induces guilt. Combine this emotion with anger and shame at the egregious behavior of the ruling party, and the resultant emotional mix fuels a moral courage that compels dissent and defiance. In Frenkel's case, this entails taking photographs, often at considerable personal risk.

In trying to understand Frenkel's evolution from physicist to photographer, it is helpful to look at his early, formative influences. His family is Jewish, and his father is a Yiddish scholar and translator who photographed his suppressed religion and culture during the Communist era. Jewish religious holidays were forbidden and therefore celebrated secretly. Frenkel Senior documented this underground resistance to Soviet orthodoxy, activities that came with their own risks. For example, his work provides a pictorial record of the life of refuseniks, Jews who were persecuted by the state for wanting to emigrate to Israel. They were fired from their jobs and unable to find equivalent positions because the only employer in a Communist system was the government. Highly educated citizens were thus forced into menial positions to avoid being arrested as "social parasites," the Soviet label for those who were unemployed and therefore not con-tributing to the state. Refuseniks found themselves in this purgatory for years.

By the time David Frenkel was born, the era of the refuseniks was largely over. If his love of photography was sparked by his father, his commitment to human rights comes from a family ethos of tolerance that includes support for Russia's LGBTQ community. It was in relation to photographing a LGBTQ rally backing workers' rights that Frenkel fell victim to another relic from the Soviet's old playbook for suppressing dissent, namely their coopting of psychiatry. A 2016 rally on Nevsky Prospekt, St. Petersburg's storied thoroughfare, was disrupted by activists from the National Liberation Movement (NLM), supporters of Putin. They attacked Frenkel too, punching and kicking him and trying to break his camera. The attack was captured on video. When Frenkel subsequently filed a complaint with the police, he was promptly arrested and accused of impeding the NLM protesters. Caught unawares by the LGBTQ protest, the police threatened Frenkel with incarceration in a psychiatry

The physicist-turned-photographer edits photographs at home.

ward if he did not divulge information on the rally's organizers.

Frenkel had every reason to take this threat seriously. Three years earlier, activist Mikhail Kosenko, who had a history of depression, was sentenced to enforced psychiatric detention and treatment for joining a protest against Putin the day before the president's third inauguration. Despite widespread outrage at the decision, the conviction was upheld on appeal. This purloining of psychiatry had reached its apotheosis under Soviet rule when psychiatric wards, called psikhushkas, were used to confine political dissidents who were often forcefully medicated with antipsychotic drugs. A discredited psychiatric diagnosis, sluggish schizophrenia, formulated by Dr. Andrei Snezhnevsky at the Moscow School of Psychiatry, was so conveniently vague that perceived resistance to the state was deemed evidence of mental illness. Psychiatric documentation from that era made reference to individuals who would appear quite normal for much of the time before showing evidence of "inflexibility of convictions" or "reformist delusions." Thousands of dissidents fell victim to this medical abuse.

When Frenkel refused to divulge information of the LGBTQ march to the police, a call was made to psychiatric services and an ambulance with three male psychiatric orderlies arrived. In the struggle that ensued, Frenkel was grabbed around the neck by one of the orderlies—"strangled" is how he described it to me—while the other two forcefully tied his hands together with cloth. What worried Frenkel more than his physical assault, however, were the accompanying verbal threats that he would be injected and detained in a psikhushka. There were antisemitic overtones to the assault, as well—snide remarks from the police about his surname being unusual for a Russian. The traumatic, sordid episode ended with the arrival of Frenkel's father, future wife, and a group friends. In the era of Brezhnev and Andropov, their presence would have counted for little. But in the Russia of today, despite recidivist tendencies, permission was sought from

Frenkel's father to have his son taken away for psychiatric assessment. He refused and his son was released.

An attempt by Frenkel to bring charges against the police and medical personnel who had assaulted him came to nothing. Russian courts refused to hear his case. Instead, he was informed that he had "behaved strangely" while in custody and that the psychiatric orderlies had been dispatched for his own safety. This approach, according to Frenkel, provides a loophole that allows these abuses to continue. Deem the person a threat to himself and then restrain him for his own protection. Frenkel's complaint is now before the European Court of Justice, where it languishes.

Frenkel's difficulties as a journalist did not end with his near escape from psychiatric confinement. He had been working at the time as a freelance photographer on assignment for *Kommersant*, a nationally distributed daily newspaper. Their management offered him no support and were incensed at having their name associated with him and his arrest. Being a freelancer meant that he had no accreditation documents on him when detained. This was held against him as evidence of unprofessional conduct. While some voices on social media were supportive, others, including those of colleagues, implied that good journalists were not beaten. In time, as the fragile state of press freedom in Russia deteriorated further, a number of these same critics would feel the force of police batons too.

The whole episode left Frenkel feeling angry. It also galvanized him to make two important changes. The first was to narrow his journalistic focus by shifting his interest from news in general to only those stories involving police brutality and human rights abuses. The second was to find a news agency that would be more supportive than *Kommersant*. His choice settled on MediaZona, the online media outlet founded by Maria Alyokhina and Nadezhda Tolokonnikova, two members of the Russian feminist punk-rock and performance art group Pussy Riot. Convicted in 2012 of "hooliganism," Alyokhina and

Frenkel cleans his cameras at home.

Tolokonnikova had spent almost two years in prison during which they reportedly endured slave-like conditions including sixteen-hour work days sewing police uniforms. Frenkel was offered the position of staff photographer by the outlet's editor, Sergey Smirnov, who in February 2021 was sentenced to twenty-five days of "administrative arrest" at an immigration detention center for re-Tweeting a joke about an upcoming antigovernment protest.

Frenkel draws a distinction between his actions as a photographer and what he considers far more courageous behavior displayed by Russian journalists covering the restive northern Caucasus region, citing the investigative reporting of the *Novaya Gazeta* journalist Elena Milashina, who has been attacked and has received death threats, including one from Chechen leader Ramzan Kadyrov. To be sure, there is a continuum of risk. At one extreme, there is Milashina and her colleague, Anna Politkovskaya, the author of *Putin's Russia: Life in a Failing Democracy*, who also chronicled human rights abuses committed by Russian forces and Chechen rebels in the second Chechen War, and who was murdered in a contract killing. But what Frenkel does not say is that his life would undoubtedly be safer and financially less stressed if he confined his work to physics, his profession by training. He has, however, chosen a different path. "When election monitors get beaten, you cannot sit by and watch," he told me. "You cannot close your eyes." And so he finds himself traversing this continuum of risk "a few steps behind the northern Caucasus" in his estimation, but "heading in the same direction."

Philp Roth has written of "family as the maker of character, family as the primary, shaping influence [and the] unending relevance of childhood." Decades back, David Frenkel's father picked up a camera to document a suppressed religion and a dying culture. His son now focuses his lens to record a subjugated democracy and the human rights abuses that are the signature of a repressive regime. Are these choices linked? One cannot be certain, but there is much wisdom in Roth's wise observation.

What is certain is that all these decisions are, in large measure, driven by a moral imperative. Father and son, photographers by conviction, not training, have kept their eyes and camera shutters open, capturing not only the dark moments in their shared history, but the resilience of the human spirit in refusing to buckle.

Democracy and the media in Russia have been under siege for years. The awarding of the 2021 Nobel Peace Prize to *Novaya Gazeta*'s editor Dmitry Muratov (shared with Philippine journalist Maria Ressa) has not changed this. Russia is rated 150 out of 180 countries by Reporters Without Borders on their index of press freedom, where it has been firmly entrenched for years. Frenkel's history helps explain why. It also reveals, in a more uplifting way, the impotence behind state-sanctioned brutality. Crude force can surely break bones. But in rare individuals, it cannot dent moral courage. A beaten and pilloried physicist-turned-photographer is testimony to that.

Left: *Marquez outside a safe house where alleged drug traffickers were spotted by members of the navy, prompting a heavy armed confrontation.* Right: *Razo in front of the Antimonumenta, a symbol of the feminist struggle that has been built in various places across the country as a protest against femicide and gender violence. Veracruz, Mexico.*

Victoria Razo and Felix Marquez

Mexican photojournalists Victoria Razo and Felix Marquez live together and on occasion work together, as well. They are young, energetic, and their work is imbued with a mission. Neither were trained as journalists. Razo took photography, while Marquez studied communications. He gravitated to photojournalism first. They met at university eight years ago when Razo went to a presentation given by a group of photojournalists, one of whom was Marquez. They now share an apartment two blocks from the beach, where the waters are warm and the sea breezes balmy. These days, there is enough work, and their skills with a camera ensure they are in demand.

But like much in present-day Mexico, first impressions obscure a parallel reality. There is a long, dark stain that runs through Mexican society. Over 79,000 people have disappeared—the majority since 2006—and Razo and Marquez have set themselves the daunting, dangerous task of photographing part of this national tragedy. Their focus is on human rights abuses and the murdered and disappeared of Veracruz. Razo has a specific interest in women who have met this fate. Marquez also photographs migrants, those who fall prey to the drug cartels and the traffickers known as coyotes.

Mexico is considered the most dangerous country in the Western hemisphere for journalists. Some states are more hazardous than others, and Veracruz is the most dangerous of them all. Since 2003, twenty-nine journalists have been killed in the state and eight have gone missing—and are presumed dead.

Above: Marquez working during an election day that turned violent.

The story of the mass graves of Colinas de Santa Fe in Veracruz has been told before in the *Globe and Mail* by journalist Stephanie Nolen, with additional reporting and photographs by Marquez. The collusion of drug cartels, local law enforcement officials, and politicians—including former Veracruz governor Javier Duarte—created a culture of impunity that enabled unfettered murder and extortion, and which continues to deny justice to the bereaved. The general lawlessness has included the relentless killing and intimidation of journalists. To counter this grave threat, sixty journalists from twenty-five international media outlets came together to pursue the stories of their murdered colleagues in the Cartel Project, an unprecedented collaborative venture with the French nonprofit organization, Forbidden Stories. Their message to the assassins was defiant: "Killing the journalist won't kill the story."

Organizations such as the Committee to Protect Journalists continue to highlight the plight of Mexican journalists. What is lesser known, however, are the psychological consequences of this work for the media in Mexico and what factors drive the determination of some journalists to keep exposing the atrocities despite the personal risks this entails. For Razo, the imperative is a dreadful statistic: ten women are murdered every day in Mexico. "The story is all around me," she told me. "You cannot turn away from it." Given the complicity of the police and local politicians in the violence, it is important for Razo that these stories are told independently of the government's official line.

Marquez feels a similar responsibility. "When people are murdered in front of your home, you become part of the violence—you are no longer an outsider; you are living it," he explained. In 2015, he began covering the unfolding Colinas de Santa Fe story. A year before, a group of eight mothers known as the Colectivo Solecito, banding together for support, had begun digging at sites rumored to be the graves of their missing children. Marquez recalls that when they found human remains, the attorney-general of Veracruz,

Razo photographing a demonstration protesting the murder of Monse Bendimes by her boyfriend.

Luis Angel Bravo Contreras, dismissed the find as dog bones. Undeterred, the mothers persisted—within 3 years, another 22,000 bones, including 298 skulls, would be unearthed.

Marquez's photographs did not sit well with the Veracruz government. He was warned off by the secretary of public security, Arturo Bermúdez Zurita. Then-governor Duarte accused him of trying to arm citizens for self-defense. That same year, his friend and fellow photojournalist Ruben Espinosa, known for his work covering social movements, fled Veracruz for Mexico City after he reported being followed and harassed. According to Marquez, Governor Duarte had become incensed after an unflattering photograph that Espinosa had taken of him appeared on the front cover of *Proceso*, a weekly left-leaning magazine. The move did not save Espinosa, who was murdered in July 2015, alongside four women.

After Espinosa's death, Marquez remembers thinking: "They are coming for me now." He was so fearful of the same fate, he did not leave his apartment for fifteen days. When he next stepped out his front door, it was to go into exile in Chile, where he remained for a year, only returning to Veracruz after an arrest warrant had been issued for the governor. Upon his return, he picked up where he left off. "Turning away, doing something else would be irresponsible," he believed. "I just cannot do it. I want Veracruz to change—not to be a negative statistic."

Navigating danger to get the photograph is only part of the challenge facing Razo and Marquez. Entering the lives of the bereaved, whose pain is ineffable, is another. The relationships Razo has developed with some of the mothers whose daughters have been murdered or disappeared can be emotional and intense. Some must surely see in her the future denied their children. Marquez, for his part, relates to the migrants. His period of exile sensitized him to their pain because he, too, has experienced some of it.

Another poignant aspect of his work are the artefacts of murdered journalists

Monse Bendimes, for whom this demonstration was held, was murdered by her boyfriend.

brought to him by their families. He photographs them as a means of remembrance. These meager objects give him insights into just how hard the lives of some of his dead colleagues were. It is heartbreaking for him to see that these slain photographers were doing this dangerous work for a pittance—using inferior cameras with parts missing, because they were just too poor to buy something better or have them repaired.

To offset the stress and pain that comes with this work, Razo has learned to unplug from her camera and distract herself with video games, rollerblading, and skating lessons. Marquez has not always been able to follow his partner's example. He has turned to psychotherapy and found it helpful.

In analyzing the factors that motivate Marquez and Razo to pursue such challenging, dangerous work, it is notable that both cite their inability to look away, to ignore morally egregious behavior. Failing to expose the vicious pique of a powerful politician whose vanity has been upset, or averting one's lens from the dehumanizing treatment of women, are not options for them.

Their moral compass, set to an uncompromising standard of decency, keeps at bay the fate that befell the central character of an Albert Camus novel. In the midst of a global COVID-19 pandemic, Camus's *The Plague* resonates more strongly than ever, but it is in his later novel, *The Fall*, that the consequences of moral injury—of inaction in response to a life-and-death situation—are laid bare. A lawyer, witness to a woman jumping from a bridge in Paris, fails to come to her aid. Beset by guilt, his life thereafter inexorably unravels.

Individuals differ widely in where they set their moral compass, of course. The brutal behavior of the cartels and coyotes and the connivance of some police and politicians in the tragedy of the murdered and disappeared people of Mexico arouse the moral indignation of a nation and a global community. Widespread sympathy for the families is mixed with anger directed at the perpetrators and, for some in Mexico, there is a sense of national shame. While

Razo and Marquez photograph the impact of a cyclone off the coast of Veracruz.

Marquez holding work-related objects of his murdered colleagues, Guillermo Luna and Gabriel Huge, which are part of Marquez's photographic memorial project Vestiges.

these emotions are common and readily understandable in response to morally unacceptable behaviors (acts of commission), what is more complex are the emotions that can follow doing nothing (acts of omission).

How far should the individual citizen go in doing something that challenges murder, coverups, and obfuscation, particularly when action can lead to peril? Here, the moral compass swings widely. Most people, while appalled at such events, do nothing other than keep their heads down, hoping that the endemic violence passes them by. A smaller segment of the population expresses their outrage through collective action, such as joining a mass march to protest the dead and missing women. Razo notes that just such an action was taken as a personal affront by President Andrés Manuel López Obrador, who pilloried women protestors by accusing them of being hired to attack the police.

Fewer still are the number who, as individuals, pursue a course of action that lifts the lid on this national tragedy, despite the potential for serious personal repercussions. It is here, along the far end of a continuum of responses, that we find grieving parents, human rights activists, law enforcement officials untainted by corruption, and a select group of journalists.

If courageous action for that rare breed of person is their antidote to moral injury, it is important to recognize that such a response is not invariable. It is, in Marquez's case, calculated, his actions always weighed against the risks they entail. Not every atrocity is filmed, not every crime exposed. Some are simply too dangerous to reveal. It is a constant struggle, he admitted—self-censorship versus the drive to tell the story. So grave are the dangers, he has seen many colleagues leave journalism "to open a taco stand in the U.S. or drive a cab." He does not judge them for this. After all, he reminded me, he fled to Chile in 2015 when fearing for his life.

Underpinning the photography of Razo and Marquez is the pressing need for widespread social change: Safe streets, diminished cartels, less corruption, untainted justice, accountable politicians, respect for women, a press unshackled from fear—in short, the basic building blocks of a functioning civil society. The moral imperative for this—and, by extension, the desire to avoid, or limit, the consequences of moral injury—is not center stage in their consciousness. Indeed, not once during my interview with them did they spontaneously mention it playing a part in motivating what they do. But it is there, subtly yet powerfully percolating in the background—unrecognized, influencing decisions, guiding reactions and responses with profound consequences for them and the subjects of their photographs. How else to explain their inability to look the other way and divert their lenses from the murdered and missing of their beautiful country?

Listening to Razo and Marquez tell me of the meaning they derive from their work reminded me of the memorable lines that come at the end of the animated film version of Ryzard Kapuściński's *Another Day of Life*. In 1976, Angola has just shed her colonial shackles. Augustino Neto's socialist MPLA movement, with Cuban help, has seen off the invading South African army. Kapuściński covered the war from the MPLA side, with whom his sympathies lay. Some of the combatants who were killed had become his friends. We see him sorting through their photographs as he reflects on the loss and how he should respond as a journalist.

"You must save something if you can, because people disappear without a trace—completely and irretrievably. First from the world, and then from our memory."

And as Kapuściński works, he imagines what the dead ask of us, the living:

"I was here.

This is how I looked.

This is the face I had when I was alive.

Look at me for a moment before you turn to something else."

Kishore. Dhaka, Bangladesh.

Ahmed Kabir Kishore

On the afternoon of May 2, 2020, Ahmed Kabir Kishore lay down for a nap. Just before sunset, a group of plainclothes security agents broke down his front door. He was told to get dressed while they went through his computers, confiscating his hard drives containing years of research. Another dozen or so agents arrived and Kishore was blindfolded, handcuffed, and driven to a holding area that smelled heavily of gas. Then he was assaulted. Still blindfolded, he was transferred to an air-conditioned building that stank of stale sweat and cigarette smoke. Twelve hours into his ordeal, his blindfold was finally removed and the reason for his detention revealed. His cartoons depicting Bangladesh's bungled response to the COVID-19 pandemic had upset the authorities.

Kishore (like most cartoonists, he uses only one name) has published four books of cartoons in his native Bangladesh, where his work has appeared widely in periodicals. His cartoons, which encompass social commentary, a fierce critique of intolerance and corruption, and the lampooning of powerful people, are never likely to sit well with a thin-skinned government.

The highest purpose of laughter, its sacramental reason for being, declared Philip Roth, is to bury wickedness in ridicule. Perhaps this can explain why a posse of seventeen men had been dispatched to deal with a cartoonist. Kishore's problems, however, were only just beginning. The beatings continued over many hours, he told me. A blow to the side of his head burst an eardrum and he lost hearing in the ear. He was not given regular medication for his diabetes. And being diabetic

Above: *Kishore's cartoons appear widely and don't sit well with the government.*

left him vulnerable to infections—a wound turned septic.

Three days after his arrest, Kishore was brought together with his friend, the dissident writer Mushtaq Ahmed. He, Kishore, and nine other individuals had all been arrested under the government's draconian Digital Security Act and accused of spreading rumors and misinformation on Facebook about COVID-19. The act has been widely criticized by human rights groups. Instituted in theory to address cybercrime, it has been wielded unscrupulously by the government to muzzle its critics. Ahmed, too, had been tortured, Kishore said, with electric shocks to his genitals.

The two detainees were handed over to the Rapid Action Battalion, a shadowy paramilitary group accused of carrying out hundreds of extrajudicial killings since its formation in 2004. They were transferred to Dhaka Central Jail, Keraniganj, where they were placed in fifteen-day quarantine with six other detainees in a six-by-eight-foot room. One of the men had a hacking cough. None were tested for COVID-19. From there, Kishore and Ahmed were moved to

different cells. Ten months of detention followed. The two men were denied bail on six occasions. It was only after Ahmed died in custody on February 25, 2021, aged fifty-three, that Kishore was granted bail. He emerged from prison in poor health. His reprieve may well be temporary; Bangladesh ranks 152 out of 180 countries on a global index of press freedom.

Kishore's brother, Ahsan Kabir, has written that Kishore acquired meningitis as an infant and needed surgery for complications from the infection, noting his sibling was "free-spirited" since his youth. Kishore, however, describes a happy childhood, growing up with five sisters and his brother in a loving family that prized the arts. His school curriculum was supplemented by the eclectic literary tastes of his father, who introduced him to the novels of Maxim Gorky, James Joyce, and John Steinbeck, among many others. When Kishore and his siblings excelled at school, they were rewarded with *MAD* magazines and the Asterix and Tintin comic books. Thus began his love of cartoons. So enamored was he of the characters that he began copying them,

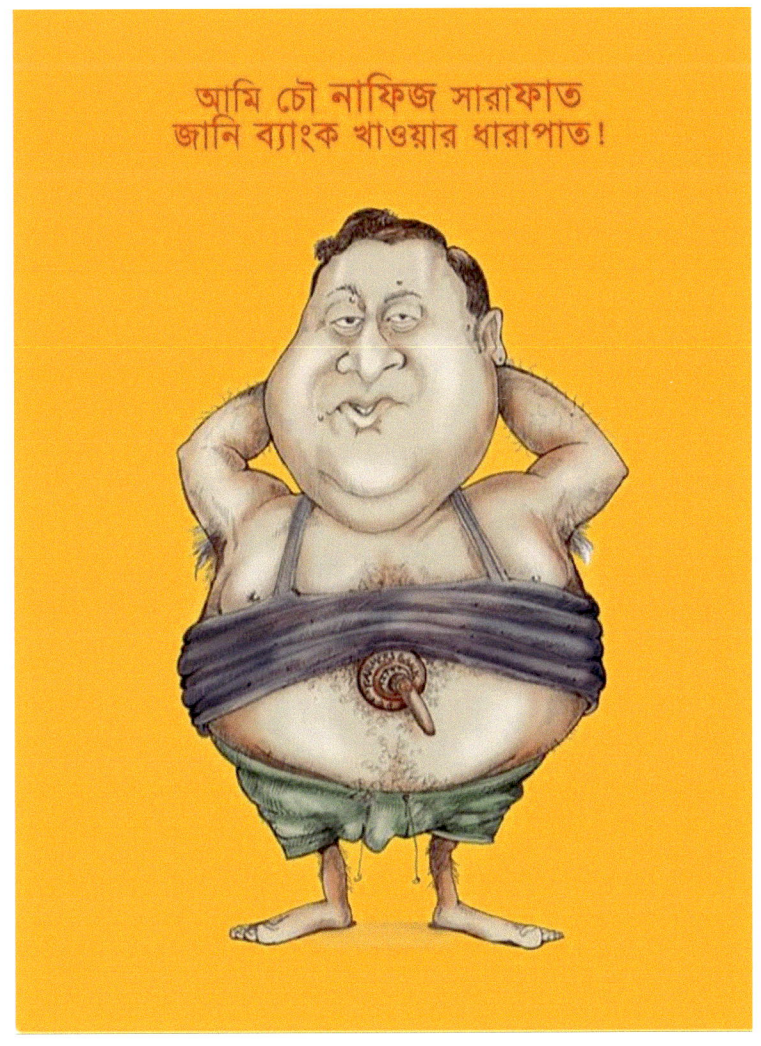

"I am Chowdhury Nafeez Sharafat who knows the ins and outs of eating up a bank" reads the caption above this caricature of the Farmers Bank chairman. A scandal involving the bank and its chairman saw vast sums of money disappear.

encouraged by his brother and with help from his father, a skilled artist.

The childhood idyll came to an abrupt end, as it so often does, with the demands of the adult world. Kishore had gained admission to university to study architecture, but the family's precarious finances meant that he had to leave his studies to find work after his first semester. He chose the one employer that guaranteed a good, steady wage and the opportunity for upward social mobility, joining the Bangladesh Defense Force and entering the navy. He obtained his bachelor of science degree through the navy and was awarded the "Captain's Cake" for his outstanding artistic ability. A photograph captures the award ceremony: Kishore in his immaculate all-white midshipman's uniform shaking the hand of Bazlur Rahman, commandant of the Bangladesh Naval Academy, the beribboned boxed cake between them.

Kishore's brief naval career, however, quickly unraveled after that, scuppered by his love of cartoons. Just before his passing-out ceremony, a number of caricatures that Kishore had drawn of his superior officers, including Commandant Rahman, came to light. His punishment was swift and severe—and a harbinger of what lay in wait for him should his talent again provoke those in power. He was forced to lug around a pack of eight bricks to the point of exhaustion, following which he was summarily kicked out of the navy.

After completing a business management program through Dhaka University, Kishore put his artistic abilities to work. Over the years, he worked for a number of advertising agencies as a copywriter and creative director, only to resign each time over what he saw as their questionable ethical practices. His moral compass was better suited to the NGO world, where he has done work for Oxfam, ActionAid International, USAID, and the Population Council, among others. Imbued with a strong idealism, and coming from a family that prized education—his wife and five sisters are all educators—he left Dhaka in 2017 and founded his own school in Khulna, his birthplace. It was to be a place of learning that recognized and nurtured the innocence and creativity of children, free of what Kishore saw as government-driven cultural suppression. He poured his own resources into this endeavor, but his passionate intensity was not enough to keep the school going.

Looking back over his life and the course it has taken, Kishore has come to see his social activism as something he "inherited." As a child, he had accompanied his father to protests against drug dealers pushing Yaba, colorful pills of amphetamine and caffeine, to the youth in their neighborhood. During his brief stint at university, he recalls being affronted by the coercive, bullying behavior of members of Islamic groups like Jamaat-e-Islami, Bangladesh's largest Islamic party. He joined protests against them, which were successful in having the group removed from campus.

Religious sensitivities surfaced again in 2007 when Kishore came to the assistance of fellow cartoonist Arifur Rahman, whose cartoon had shown a boy calling his cat "Muhammad Cat" because of the Muslim custom of putting Muhammad before a male given name. Published in a satirical supplement to the daily newspaper *Prothom Alo*, the cartoon provoked outrage among Muslim groups, leading to large protests against the newspaper, the firing of the supplement's deputy editor, and Rahman being taken into custody and charged with damaging religious sentiment. Kishore repeatedly visited his colleague in custody during his six months of detention and ultimately helped him leave Bangladesh for political asylum in Norway. When Rahman's mother took gravely ill while her son was in exile, Kishore organized, at considerable personal expense, a two-day cartoon exhibit to raise money for her medical care.

William Hogarth, the eighteenth-century English painter, printmaker, pictorial satirist, and social critic, is Kishore's "philosophical guru." In particular, he cites Hogarth's *Emblematic Print on the South Sea Scheme*, which depicts vast financial malfeasance, as the inspiration for some of his work exposing corruption in Bangladesh. Given Bangladesh's reputation as a plutocracy, there are rich pickings for a cartoonist. One example entailed Kishore cleverly depicting a scandal involving the Farmers Bank and its chairman Chowdhury Nafeez

Kishore posting on social media.

Sharafat, in which vast sums of money disappeared. Sharafat, who is well connected to Prime Minister Sheikh Hasina, reportedly is known as "The Bank Eater of Bangladesh," and Kishore's powerful cartoon shows the decidedly portly chairman with his vest rolled up, exposing a large belly with a navel that has been replaced by the combination lever to a bank vault.

While holding down his day job, Kishore kept at his cartoons, using them as a vehicle for supporting social issues, such as LGBTQ rights and the plight of the hijras, Bangladesh's transgender community. The dangers of doing so were painfully exposed by the murder of a colleague, Xulhaz Mannan, the editor of Bangladesh's first LGBTQ magazine, *Roopbaan*. Kishore has also focused on the grave hazards faced by his country's secular blogger community, some of whom have been hacked to death by religious fundamentalists on the streets, often in broad daylight.

Kishore notes that his cartoons are visual representations of current events. He is at pains to emphasize that he sticks to the facts and does not fabricate them by claiming artistic license. His work ethic calls to mind a couple of Will Rogers's witticisms: "I don't make jokes—I just watch the government and report the facts" and "there is no trick to being a humorist when you have the whole government working for you." In Bangladesh's case, the humor is dark more often than not. Death hovers.

Kishore's work has made an impact not just in his home country, but around the world. He was recognized by *Unmad*, Bangladesh's only satire magazine, with their first Unmad Medal in 2005. In 2020, he received the Robert Russell Courage in Cartooning Award from the nonprofit Cartoonists Rights Network International (CRNI), which applauded his contribution to social engagement and the defense of human rights. While in detention, he was supported by Amnesty International, which paid his legal costs. CRNI also supported him financially after his incarceration. Following his release in February, he was given an artist-in-residence position at Drik (or "vision" in Sanskrit) Picture Library in Dhaka, founded by photographer and writer Shahidul Alam, who has also been detained and tortured for his commitment to social change.

When Kishore's friends, concerned for his safety, tell him to take a break from his activism, he responds by asking them, "Until when?" Having concluded the government will not change, his work continues, driven by his conviction that "the world must become more human."

Displaying moral courage has come at great personal cost to Kishore. "I don't belong to this country. I don't belong to my family," he said pointedly. He lives alone now, separated from his ex-wife—the couple divorced when he was in jail—and their daughter. He no longer has contact with his five sisters and minimal contact with his brother. He believes their telephone calls are monitored, and one of his greatest fears is that his family will be targeted as a way of getting to him. With a bitter laugh, he wryly told me that as opportunities for contact with his family have been closed off, his friendships, "Facebook friends," have greatly increased, courtesy of his time in prison.

Kishore is a kindly, compassionate man with a creative gift. The material world means little to him. He has shown boundless generosity to friends and strangers. His principles, which reveal a naiveté both touching and at times self-defeating, are the antithesis of the path followed by conniving, corrupt, and cynical politicians. An intolerant government wielding vast powers under cover of a dubious law has set out to silence this gentle soul. They have succeeded in undermining his fragile physical health. Prolonged detention and beatings have left him psychologically traumatized. But there is one aspect to the cartoonist's being that appears impervious to the malign forces arrayed against him: his moral courage.

Kishore's core beliefs have never wavered. Out on bail and facing an unpredictable, dangerous future, the one certainty is his steadfast moral compass. Give him a pencil and some paper, and he will follow his lodestar. This is what punitive authorities know and fear. Moral courage does not lessen his own fear. And knowing all of this, we fear for him, too.

Bido in her garden at home, an oasis in contrast to the war torn streets outside. Idlib, Syria.

Yakeen Bido

The numbers alone tell a grim story. Since peaceful protests against the regime of Bashar al-Assad began in Syria in 2011, around 400,000 people have been killed—including more than 12,000 children—with 5.6 million Syrians becoming refugees and 6.2 million now internally displaced. It is estimated that the government has executed between 5,000 and 13,000 of its citizens and tortured many more to death. The future of this shattered country remains uncertain while the final chapter in a ruinous decade-long civil war has yet to be written.

Amid the charnel house of Syria today is the city of Idlib, 328 kilometers northwest of the capital Damascus. It is the last remaining major city in Syria that has resisted the army of President al-Assad.

The dominant rebel group governing Idlib and surrounding regions is Hayat Tahrir al-Sham (HTS), an offshoot of the Al-Nusra Front, which had declared allegiance to Al-Qaeda early in the war. Since 2016, HTS has tried to distance itself from its jihadist origins, but suspicions about its true ideological bent remain. While Canada no longer considers it a terrorist entity, the United States still does.

Idlib is home to Yakeen Bido, a twenty-seven-year-old freelance journalist and relentless chronicler of her country's agony. Bido was only eighteen when the Arab Spring first came to Syria. She had just begun her sociology studies at Tishreen University in Lakatia, commuting from her family home in Idlib—a journey that became increasingly fraught as the

Above: *Bido shows a girl her photograph at a refugee tent encampment.*

Bido working on her laptop in a coffee shop.

civil unrest spread and the government's responses turned more draconian.

The citizens of Idlib had joined the protests against the Assad regime, and Bido recalls the government soldiers manning multiple checkpoints along her route calling her a terrorist and threatening to burn Idlib and turn the verdant green of the region brown, yellow, and black. At one point, she was arrested and held for four hours, damned by association with the city of her birth. When government forces attacked Idlib in 2012, her family home was torched and one of her brothers and some cousins briefly detained.

Syria's descent into civil war brought a premature end to Bido's university studies. Rather than bemoan a lost career, she saw the chance to reinvent herself in the seething mayhem of revolutionary life. Equipped with basic journalistic skills acquired during her aborted studies, she resolved to tell the stories of her fellow citizens who were being harassed and arrested—and who, in some cases, had dis-appeared. Her background as a sociology student guided her choice of subjects at first, so she focused on the cultural and social aspects of the conflict. Her reportage has appeared on BBC-TV, France 24, Damascus Voice Radio, Al-Kul Radio, and other notable media outlets.

The prolonged civil war has deprived a generation of Syrian children of their childhood. Bido was only a teenager when the war first began. In a society at peace, the transition from child to adult—that watershed developmental period—is allowed time and space to progress.

War put an end to all of that for Bido's generation in Syria. Robbed of her adolescence, she found herself overnight inhabiting the nightmare world of adults caught up inextricably in civil war. Acutely aware of her lost years, Bido says it's part of the reason why she is so determined to inform her fellow citizens and the world at large of the effects of aerial bombing and Russian artillery barrages on Idlib's youth. "I was one of them," she poignantly observes.

A regime that has used chemical weapons multiple times on its own people is unlikely to welcome investigative reporting. For two consecutive years, Syria has ranked 174 out of 180 countries on an index of press freedom according to international NGO Reporters Without Borders. In keeping with its pariah status, the Assad regime has sanctioned the targeted assassination of journalists—including, among others, the celebrated American correspondent Marie Colvin, killed while covering the siege of Homs for the *Sunday Times* in 2012.

Bido was aware that a government brazen enough to murder a high-profile journalist such as Colvin would have little hesitancy going after someone like her. Mindful of the danger, she initially adopted the nom de plume Mirna al-Hassan for her reporting. Such a simple ruse, however, was never going to dupe the ubiquitous ears and eyes of a police state, and she soon reverted to using her own name. As she anticipated, the attacks were not long in coming. "I am what they call 'wanted' by the Assad regime," she says. "I have been targeted by all means possible."

Criminal gangs and repressive regimes use a common playbook in their attempts to intimidate the press. The drug cartels of Mexico and the Ayatollahs of Iran, to mention but two incongruous bedfellows, try to break journalists by going after their families. The Syrian government is no different. A bomb was left at the entrance of the gas station owned by Bido's father and one of her brothers. Neither was injured in the explosion, but the message was clear. That incident was followed by an attack on her car—while she wasn't in the vehicle at the time, there was no mistaking the intent.

Online abuse came next: the Assad regime claimed that she had been raped and that her father had expelled her from the family as a result. This smear, playing into deeply held traditional beliefs about a woman's "honor," was meant to shame not only Bido, but her entire family. While the attempt failed on both accounts, by

Bido is the only woman journalist who has been reporting continuously from Idlib since 2015.

bringing sex into the intended shaming, it highlighted not only Bido's vulnerability as a woman in a war zone, but also her unique profile as one of the few local female journalists covering the Syrian revolution.

Bido is the only woman who has been reporting uninterruptedly from within Idlib since 2015, when the city was retaken from the Assad regime. Other Syrian female journalists have come to Idlib to report the war but have left. She alone has stayed, apart from a three-month period in 2015 when her neighborhood came under intense shelling and she and her family had to take refuge in a nearby village.

Bido has also used her presence to refute the Assad government's propaganda that Idlib is controlled by Islamists. She recalls the battle for the village of Saraqib, 16 kilometers from Idlib. When the village was captured by the Free Syrian Army, she made and broadcast a video standing alongside her male colleagues—something, she points out, that would not have been sanctioned by a fundamentalist movement like ISIS or Al-Qaeda. "I am a thorn in the throat of the Assad regime," she says.

More than a third of Bido's young life has been under the shadow of war amid the barrel bombs, artillery barrages, and indiscriminate shelling of Assad's army and his Russian, Iranian, and Hezbollah proxies. Describing the emotional effects of such prolonged exposure to extreme violence, she is at pains to underscore the collective nature of suffering in Idlib. "Yes, I have nightmares," she confided, "all the time. But not only me! I see nightmares at night and nightmares during the day. *We* in Idlib have gotten used to this. It is the sounds of shelling and air raids that cannot escape my ears. Yes, Idlib is free now, but *we* live in constant fear of Assad and his Russians. There are so many martyrs, so many in jail—who will be next? The people of Idlib live in constant agony over their past, present, and future," she adds. "*We* worry constantly. Therefore, *we* hardly sleep."

Bido is relentless in her coverage of the conflict and how it has pummelled her hometown. "Death is at my doorstep," she tells me. "I do not think about it a lot. It is our fate." Remarkable words from a person so young. One must have endured much to reach such an acceptance, which also explains why her hopes for the future are expressed in such visceral, lacerating language. "I dream of the day when we get rid of the dictator Bashar al-Assad, the snake in the body of every Syrian."

When explaining what motivates her to continue pursuing such dangerous work, it is clear Bido strongly identifies with her fellow citizens in their struggle. This intense drive for freedom is one part of the antidote to her periods of depression. The other is her need to bear witness. At times, she says, she feels overwhelmed by the magnitude of suffering she has seen: "the blood on people's faces after a massacre, all the body parts, the screaming of the women during the shelling." But such horror is also her spur to action, she explains. People tell her that her coverage is important and necessary. "They never stop encouraging me,"

she says, adding that helps pull her out of despondency and despair.

When asked if she had ever considered leaving Syria, her immediate, incandescent response is revealing: "I will never leave, because I do not want to miss the smell of the graves—the smell of the dead, the pictures of the dead, of the dear ones who we have lost in this revolution. If I leave, then the hope of keeping Idlib free will disappear. For the hope of others—and my own hope—I must stay with my neighbors, with my family."

This intrepid journalist sees her reportage as her contribution to the ongoing struggle of everyday Syrians. Like her fellow citizens, she has lost too much to change course. A beloved brother was killed—"martyred by the Assad regime" is how she describes his death, declining to elaborate, as reliving the incident is simply too painful.

As our interview drew to a close, I chose a question that I thought would evoke a different reply from her, a softer one perhaps, recalling happier memories of things past. "What had life been like in Idlib during her childhood, before the revolution?" I wanted to know. Her answer was not what I expected.

"Yes, Idlib had been peaceful once," she remembers. "A small, simple city, ignored, families living together, an agricultural sector that was quite prosperous. I saw happiness." That was as far as nostalgia went. To Yakeen Bido, the Idlib of today, under siege, bombed relentlessly, home to so much death and destruction and personal heartbreak is "much nicer than the Idlib I remember as a child. Idlib is economically developed. Idlib is free from the Assad regime. Idlib is now a free area. People know about it now because it is free from the dictatorial regime."

In this response from a twenty-seven-year-old journalist who once had hoped to become a sociologist, we see why dictators are ultimately toppled and repressive regimes overthrown.

Dündar in Berlin, Germany, January 31, 2023.

Can Dündar

Over the course of his forty-year career, Turkish journalist Can Dündar has been witness to, and participant in, the competing forces that have roiled his country's recent history; secular versus religious, democracy versus authoritarianism, tolerance versus dogmatism. As a young man, he recalls considering two potential career choices—medicine and journalism—and deciding on the latter. Medicine could save one life at a time, he reasoned, whereas journalism could save the planet. Four decades on, he smiles wistfully when recollecting the passionate intensity of his youthful ideals. Time and life's hard knocks may have tempered some of his expectations, but his core belief in journalism as a force for good in a troubled society has never wavered.

Dündar was born in Ankara, Turkey. His father held an administrative position in the Turkish intelligence service while his mother worked for the Ministry of Culture, preparing press cards for journalists. When he was sixteen years of age, he responded to a call from a Turkish newspaper requesting articles that reflected how the youth saw their lives. His article, comparing the respective merits of medicine and journalism, revealed a precocious political and social awareness. Journalism was important in a country like Turkey, he explained, because it helped people by keeping them informed of what was going on. His article

Above: Dündar chose journalism as a career because he saw it as a way of contributing to civil society..

was not published, but any lingering career uncertainties were gone.

In 1978, Dündar enrolled in media studies through the department of political science at Ankara University, an institution with a long history of leftist traditions. His parents never tried to dissuade him from journalism even though the profession was not popular. "Journalists didn't earn much," he told me, "and died at sixty years of age from a heart attack if they managed to survive government aggression." He was beginning his studies at a time of major political upheaval in Turkey with resurgent street violence between leftists and nationalists.

The first two years of his four-year program were devoted to general topics, not journalism, but Dündar soon learned that if he was to find a job when he qualified, he needed to start working a lot sooner. In 1979, he was taken on as a trainee by *Yanki* ("Echo" in Turkish), a magazine, where his progress was meteoric. Within a year, he was on the editorial board. A bloodless military coup the following year, Turkey's third in twenty years, put an end to rival political factions killing one another. Up to half a million people were detained, many of whom were tortured and died in custody. The eyes of the world were on Turkey, a key NATO member occupying a crucial geopolitical niche astride the Bosphorus. The times may have been dangerous, but they were alive with opportunity for a young journalist caught up in the drama of the moment.

Dündar was aware that he was in the right place at the right time. He was still completing his studies while rubbing shoulders in newsrooms with well-known journalists, local and foreign. The atmosphere was intense, electric in keeping with history unfolding on the magazine's doorstep, and Dündar soaked it all in, observing how skilled journalists practiced their craft and learning invaluable lessons along the way.

The putsch may have brought an end to the violence on the streets, but the situation for journalists remained hazardous. On a personal level, he remembers how his political books were burned in

*Dündar, Editor in Chief of Cumhuriyet, in his office in Istanbul on February 26, 2016
after being released from jail.*

the bathroom by his father on the night the military seized power. Was this being excessively cautious? Nineteen-year-old Dündar thought so, but different generations view life-changing events through their own repositories of memory and with differing proclivities for risk.

More ominous, however, were the work restrictions he had to navigate. The military censor kept a close eye on the press. Nobody wanted to go to jail, Dündar recalls, and so it fell to him as a newly appointed editor to attend court each day and explain why *Yanki* was publishing stories viewed with suspicion by the censors. In light of the fraught nature of this work, he remembers viewing his recent promotion as "a kind of punishment."

Yanki was, however, in a more fortunate position than other media organizations. The editor-in-chief had established a good relationship with the junta. This afforded Dündar and his colleagues a degree of protection. Dündar's first award as a journalist was for an investigative report on people who had disappeared in detention while under investigation. It was a story of great emotional power—parents, desperate for news of their missing children—and it fell to a twenty-one-year-old journalist to break it.

Typically, a story like this would have been quashed, but it was not because it was balanced with a headline that reflected favorably on the army. This deft slight of hand, akin to self-censorship, came to define a dangerous pas de deux between the press and the military. Failure to play by these distorted rules risked time in jail or expulsion from the country. Such was the media landscape in Turkey as Dündar's undergraduate studies came to an end.

No sooner had Dündar qualified and been given his freshly minted press card by his mother, a touching family moment, than he concluded that his training "had not allowed me to see the world correctly." He decided to take a break from journalism, as it had become virtually impossible to get an article freely published, and immerse himself in academia. What followed was a master's degree and then a PhD through the Middle East Technical University in Ankara. The topic of his dissertation was a comparison of two controversial events, one pertaining to the United Kingdom and the sinking of the Argentine cruiser, the *Belgrano*, during the Falklands war, and the other to Turkey and the mistaken bombing of a Turkish naval ship by the country's own air force during the Turkish invasion of Cyprus. Both events were followed by government attempts to suppress key facts. The issue of government secrecy versus the public's right to know became a theme that has defined Dündar's career ever since.

With his doctorate completed, Dündar returned to journalism. In 1993, he moved to *Hurriyet*, the biggest Turkish daily, where he was their parliamentary correspondent. Along the way, he had also started to work in television, beginning with the *32nd Day* news program. By the early 1990s, journalism had become very dangerous once again. Journalists were harassed and killed, and Dündar was witness to this. On January 24, 1993, a car bomb killed the leg-endary journalist Ugur Mumcu outside his home. Dündar's office was nearby; hurrying to the scene, he came across the grisly murder site.

The assassination of a respected colleague left Dündar feeling shaken but determined to continue his work. If anything, it bolstered his resolve. "It was our responsibility to take over," he told me. He learned that Mumcu had been working on the story of a journalist murdered in 1979. Now he had met the same fate. Two journalists both murdered might have made a third journalist leery of continuing the investigation, but not Dündar. He went on to make a documentary about the killings. "When you get into the business of journalism, you must be ready for such risks," he told me. "Our prizes are bullets. That's how they reward you in a country like Turkey. That is how you know you are doing something useful for the people."

On May 28, 2013, Turkey was rocked by the Gezi Park protests. What started as a local demonstration against urban development plans for Istanbul's Taksim Gezi

Murat Sahin, who attempted to shoot prominent Turkish journalist Dündar, is held by Dilek Dündar, wife of Dündar, and an unidentified man. Dündar is seen in the background being protected by TV reporter Yagiz Senkal who was injured during the attack outside a courthouse. May 6, 2016, Istanbul, Turkey.

Park snowballed into widespread protests against a miscellany of grievances, including restrictions on freedom of the press and the erosion of Turkey's secularism by a government with an Islamist bent. Dündar was covering the protests for *Milliyet*, a daily newspaper, reporting from the park day and night. His articles were not well received by his editor and the government. To remove him from the scene, he was dispatched to cover protests that had flared in Egypt following a coup that saw the military under General el-Sisi seize power. Dündar's reportage comparing the respective situations in Egypt and Turkey annoyed the government once again and he was let go by *Milliyet*. In losing his job, he had fallen foul of yet another form of press censorship that saw Prime Minister Erdogan encouraging his rich cronies to purchase media outlets for the purpose of enforcing editorial policies that favored his government.

After leaving *Milliyet*, Dündar became the anchorman at +1TV. The channel had come into possession of damning telephone conversations, wire tapped by elements in the police opposed to the government. The calls were between Erdogan and his son, in which they discussed how to hide money at home in the event of a police search. +1TV leaked the recordings and Dündar made a documentary on the story. Not surprisingly in that political climate, +1TV could not attract advertisers. The station did not survive.

Soon thereafter, Dündar was appointed editor-in-chief of *Cumhuriyet*. The left-leaning Turkish daily had been started in 1924 by journalist Yunus Nadi Abalıoğlu, a confidant of the founder of the Turkish Republic, Mustafa Kemal Atatürk. The paper was known for promoting democratic ideals and a pluralistic, secular society. Over the years, seven of its journalists have been assassinated, including Ugur Mumcu. "When we enter the building every morning, we see their photographs," Dündar told me. "Every morning you understand again that if you touch these stories, if you write this article, this is the destiny waiting for you."

Listening to Dündar describe the stark message conveyed by these portraits of murdered colleagues reminded me of a similar display in the corridors of *Novaya Gazeta* in Moscow. There, beyond the security checkpoint, is a white corridor also lined with photographs of the dead. How different this is from the *New York Times* head office in Manhattan where a wall is adorned by photos of their Pulitzer Prize–winning journalists. The lottery of birth can cast a long shadow.

As editor-in-chief of a venerable newspaper with *Cumhuriyet*'s history, Dündar was acutely aware of the ramifications of his decisions to publish certain articles. "You can be brave for yourself," he confided in me, "but not for others. You have to think twice before endangering colleagues, family, friends, the whole newspaper." One such explosive story involved Turkey's National Intelligence Organization covertly supplying weapons to radical Islamist groups in Syria. Dündar had video proof implicating the government. The paper's lawyers advised that publishing ran the risk of the paper being raided and journalists going to jail. Dündar asked his editors for their opinion. All favored publication.

When the story broke in February 2015, an enraged President Erdogan publicly threatened Dündar by letting him know he would "pay a heavy price for this." The "price" was delayed because Turkey was going to the polls in a few months and arresting a pre-eminent journalist would not be a vote-getter. Erdogan's party, however, lost the June election. Five months of unrest and bloodshed followed. When the country went to the polls again in November, Erdogan emerged victorious. A couple of weeks later, Dündar and his Ankara bureau chief Erdem Gul were arrested on trumped up charges. Ninety-two days in prison followed before the Constitutional Court ordered their release.

On May 6, 2016, outside a courthouse in Istanbul, Dündar survived an assassination attempt unhurt. Later that day, he was sentenced to five years and ten months in jail for revealing state secrets. His would-be assassin, a member of a gang with known links to the government, was released from prison after a couple of months, a free man.

The Turkish government never condemned the attack but did assign Dündar a protection team. With an appeal pending, he continued working and traveling. He took time off from his role as editor and rented a flat in Barcelona where he finished a book. It was in Barcelona on July 15, 2016, that he learned of the failed coup attempt against President Erdogan's government. The authorities' draconian response to the insurrection saw the last vestige of an independent judiciary, the Constitutional Court, brought under Erdogan's control. It was now too dangerous for Dündar to return home.

Can Dündar has been living in exile in Berlin ever since. In 2018, the 16th Criminal Chamber of the Supreme Court of Appeals reversed his conviction on the grounds that he should have been charged with espionage instead. He was handed a twenty-seven and a half year prison sentence in abstentia. The Turkish government stripped him of all his assets. His wife's passport was confiscated. She was only able to join him three years later by slipping out of the country illegally. He is still harassed daily by elements in Germany's large expatriate Turkish community who have become even more radical and nationalistic living in the diaspora and view him as a traitor. Not all his 5.5 million Twitter followers are admirers. There are daily death threats. Police protection is provided for his public appearances.

When I asked Dündar about the emotional toll his work has taken, his response turned my question on its head: "If I have survived psychologically, it is thanks to my struggle." It is a striking answer, but behind the defiance is a more nuanced insight. "I do not feel the bleeding at the moment," he told me. "I am surrounded by too much chaos. Maybe at the end of this chaos I will understand what kind of damage I have in my heart. But for the moment, I do not have the time to think about it. I am still fighting."

The fight he alludes to is waged on

many levels. He continues working as a journalist and is editor-in-chief of OZGU-RUZ, a web-based radio station run by the not-for-profit investigative newsroom, Correctiv. But the struggle does not end there. In the past, when Dündar spoke to young journalists, he advised them to separate activism from journalism. "Unfortunately, I see it differently now," he divulged, observing that, in the West, journalists typically keep a distance from their stories. "But for people like me," he noted, "our house is burning and we hear the screams of our loved ones inside. . . . We cannot say this is not our business and just report it."

The idea of journalists transcending journalism as part of a greater struggle is one that Dündar returned to repeatedly in our interview. "In a country like Turkey, journalism has a different meaning: it is part of the powerplay. With a functioning judicial or political system, journalism would not be that important. But without it, journalism is almost the only means to expose the government's dirty secrets and change something. It is a mission, a responsibility, rather than a profession, especially nowadays."

Marching in tandem with Dündar's activism is the pain of loss. This was also alluded to repeatedly, not as a complaint but to highlight yet another challenge that he has had to confront, this time in his sixties. "I have lost everything in my life. My country, my family, my friends, my house, my car, my library, because of journalism. You can lose everything in one day and then you have to build it up again." And as he was making this point, he held up a pen for me to see. "This [pen] put me in jail and brought me to exile in Germany, but it also contributed to my life by giving me a feeling I am doing something useful." Had he kept quiet, like Erdem Gul did after they were both released from prison, his life would have followed a very different trajectory. Gul never went back to journalism, but entered politics instead and became mayor of Princes' Islands.

Staying silent was never an option for Dündar. "If I had kept quiet, I would have been destroyed," he told me. "I know peo-

Forced into exile by his refusal to stay quiet, Dündar has endured many losses.

ple who have a family and a good car and a good house without writing anything at all against this aggression and they feel horrible. Comparing their situation to mine, I chose mine."

In his choice, we see the power of moral injury determining behavior. Silence, an act of omission, with all its practical benefits is viewed as intolerable. This, more than a vengeful government, has to be avoided. To continue keeping moral injury at bay, he records two minutes of his thoughts every day in which he says things that are unspeakable in Turkey. Should he miss this short ritual, even for a day, he feels guilty. And with this admission, we see one of the primary emotions associated with moral injury—guilt—ready to rise up lest he lapse in his resolve.

Moral courage has fortified Dündar in his long and difficult quest. This imbues his journey navigating choppy, dangerous waters with a Homeric quality. As our interview wound down, this accomplished journalist, man of letters, author of multiple books, and recipient of notable honors, spoke of his hopes for the future. He dreams of returning to a country at peace. He will reunite with family and friends. He will spend time in his summer home. And there, surrounded by tranquility, he will be left to write.

Ismayilova in her office. Baku, Azerbaijan.

Khadija Ismayilova

No sooner had my interview with Azerbaijani journalist Khadija Ismayilova began than she had a request: Could we please focus on her work rather than her life? For as she noted, when people write about journalists who are harassed, they tend to forget about the essence of why they are persecuted. Framed this way, her request seemed reasonable—but when work and life become inextricably linked, as they are with her, then disentangling the threads in order to bypass a remarkable personality misses an important part of the gestalt.

Yes, her accomplishments as an investigative journalist surely stand on their own. But her life—what she has had to endure as a result of these accomplishments—elevates them still further. The whole is greater than the sum of its parts. "Unfortunately," she said ruefully, "when journalists write about the bad guys, it turns up consequences for the authors."

Ismayilova was born in an Azerbaijan that was still part of the Soviet Union. She was a schoolgirl when she joined the All-Union Leninist Young Communist League, known as Komsomol, and as a Pioneer (the league's group for those aged nine to fourteen), recalls writing poems in praise of Lenin and denouncing America. Both her parents were engineers, and her father, a member of parliament and a minister in the government of then-president Heydar Aliyev, was responsible for overseeing the country's rich oil and gas industry. She recalls their home was continually full of guests, with her parents always hosting and helping fellow citizens, their efforts part of

Above: Ismayilova in the courtyard of Toplum TV, Baku, Azerbaijan.

some greater collective good. To outsiders, the Ismayilovs must have seemed like a model Soviet family.

It took a televised soccer game between the Soviet Union and Turkey in 1986 to open young Khadija's eyes to the precarious reality of her family's true existence. Ismayilova recollects being shocked at seeing her parents supporting Turkey. When she asked what they were doing, her mother, brushing aside her husband's concerns, divulged the family's big secret: "We are actually Turks," Ismayilova remembers her saying. "Russia has occupied our country. It is the Russians, not the West, who are the imperialists." If this was not enough for a ten-year-old child to digest, her mother also let it be known that she had been a dissident in her youth. "Within ten minutes, I had learned about empire, occupation, forbidden national identity, and censorship," Ismayilova told me. A few days later, the Komsomal Pioneer burned her journals—and with them, her poems to Vladimir Ilyich Lenin.

Looking back at her childhood, Ismay-ilova remembers that everything was a secret, from listening to the BBC and Voice of America, to her mother buying Gershwin records and her grandmother going to the mosque. By the time she was a teenager, glasnost and perestroika were opening up society and the Stalinist past was being reexamined. Yet despite this newfound openness, there were certain lines in Aliyev's Azerbaijan that could not be crossed. Ismayilova's father had spoken out against corruption in high places, and after drawing attention to failings within the lucrative energy industry at a cabinet meeting broadcast live, he was summarily fired. Gone overnight and shunned by Aliyev, who governed through patronage and clan-like loyalty, he would never find a job in Azerbaijan again.

When her father was dismissed, Ismay-ilova was in her third year of university. With her mother having long left engineering to be a stay-at-home parent, the situation marked a sharp downturn in the family's fortunes. "He had always held high government office, and because he was not corrupt, we had no money," she said. "It was suddenly a challenge to buy food." Her father's precipitous fall from grace for speaking the truth would prove a portent for Ismayilova's own coming battles with the Aliyev family.

Ismayilova is not a journalist by training. She graduated from the School of Oriental Studies at Baku State University after studying Turkish philology. Fluent in Russian, Turkish, and English, she briefly found work as a translator before transitioning into journalism. Her father had wanted her to be an academic ("he had this Soviet fetish for a PhD," is how she saw it), and in deference to his wishes, she had enrolled for postgraduate studies at the Academy of Sciences in Baku, but after he died, she dropped her studies to work full-time as a journalist. "If journalism had not been so fascinating, perhaps I would have gone along with it," she recalls.

Ismayilova's early career was stormy as she joined and soon resigned from a series of Azerbaijani newspapers. Looking back at this period, she is unsparing in her self-crit-icism. "I had a bad temper, would not accept orders, made a lot of mistakes, and was too defensive," she admitted. Three years of relative job stability followed when she was appointed editor of political news for *Echo*, a Russian paper in Azerbaijan, but she resigned in protest two days after the 2003 election which saw Ilham Aliyev succeed his father Heydar as president. *Echo* was pro-government, she explained to me, and had failed to tell the truth about the new leader's corruption.

In the years that followed, Ismayilova worked for Caspian Business News covering the environment and economy, wrote for Eurasianet (a website based at Columbia University's Harriman Institute, one of the leading centers of scholarship on Eurasia), and spent eighteen months in the United States working for Voice of America before returning home to train local journalists. She later became a bureau chief for Radio Liberty (a U.S.-funded platform that reports news, information, and analysis to countries in Eastern Europe, Central Asia, Caucasus, and the Middle East) and the editor of Radio Liberty's team in Baku. While her work focused increasingly on corruption, she did not yet see herself as an investigative journalist.

The murder of Azerbaijani freelance journalist Elmar Huseynov in 2005 changed that. While it was widely believed that Huseynov was murdered to silence his criticism of Ilham Aliyev and his father, Ismayilova also saw his death as an indictment of the media in Azerbaijan. "We were partly responsible for his assassination," she told me. "He was killed because he was the only one investigating the president's family and their businesses."

In trying to understand what came next in her career, it is important to take note of Ismayilova's feeling of guilt: she experienced an allied emotion, shame, a few years later when the *Washington Post* approached her to fact check their story on the numerous Dubai properties of Ilham Aliyev's children. It transpired that Aliyev's eleven-year-old son was the owner of nine waterfront mansions valued at around $44 million USD. "I felt ashamed that foreign journalists do this work and we don't," Ismayilova remembers.

With her inquiring mind and a gimlet eye, Ismayilova began digging. She looked into the impunity afforded Huseynov's assassins. She exposed how millions of dollars had gone missing from Azerbaijan's national bank. She revealed the corrupt commercial dealings of Kamaladdin Heydarov, appointed chairman of the state customs committee by Heydar Aliyev in 1995 and minister of emergency situations by Ilham Aliyev in 2006. Heydarov's business empire, ranging from fruit juice to real estate, had garnered massive wealth for his family.

Ismayilova also began looking into the Panama Papers for links with the Azerbaijani ruling elite. At first, she lacked the technical expertise to mine this trove of millions of leaked documents that detail attorney-client information on hundreds of thousands of offshore entities. Paul Radu, cofounder of the Organized Crime and Corruption Reporting Project (OCCRP), taught her how to sort through

A poster on the wall of Ismayilova's office has a quote in Turkish from The Little Prince, which reads: "everyone has a star, but none of them is like the others."

and interpret the data. What emerged was evidence showing that the president's wife and daughter owned numerous companies.

Ismayilova also returned to a previously abandoned investigation of the cellphone company Azerphone—with her new skillset, she was now able to refute the government's lie that Azerphone was owned by global tech company Siemens. In fact, three companies listed as based in Panama were the owners—and all three belonged to Ilham Aliyev's daughter. Regulations for bids and contracts had been bypassed and licenses granted without competition or oversight.

At times, the sheer weight of corruption alone must have seemed overwhelming. Ismayilova revealed that the government had more assets outside the country than within. She exposed fraud in the 2008 national elections. She unearthed connections between the Aliyevs, construction projects, and the Eurovision Song Contest, as well as links between the Azerbaijani First Family and a bribery scandal involving Luca Volontè, an Italian deputy and member of the Parliamentary Assembly of the Council of Europe. In 2021, Volontè was sentenced to four years in prison for taking $2.43 million USD in bribes to dampen European criticism of Azerbaijan's human rights record.

No local journalist in Azerbaijan had gone this far before. The government responded by taking Radio Liberty off the air locally. In response, Ismayilova moved her program online—the government's riposte was to jam the satellite.

After Ismayilova's first Panama Papers exposé, the intimidation turned more ominous, eventually leading to blackmail. From July 2011 through January 2012, cameras were secretly placed in her apartment and she was recorded being intimate with her boyfriend. Her brother was sent stills from the video with a note calling her a whore. Azerbaijan is a very traditional society, where it is taboo for women to have sex outside of marriage. Tradition demanded of her brother that he either kill her, her boyfriend, or the person who made the video.

She recalls finding out about the video from her brother just as she was about to go on air. Remarkably, she went ahead with the program. After consulting with the OCCRP and her lawyer, she wrote a Facebook post about being blackmailed and how the tactics would not stop her work. The following day, she wrote another post listing her ongoing investigations and those in the pipeline. A week later, the Azerbaijani government released the video through a website they claimed belonged to the country's main opposition party. Ismayilova's supporters encouraged her to say the video was a fabrication, but she refused. "I owned it," she told me defiantly. She had seen the government use tactics like this before to break journalists and silence them. She would have none of it.

The government's blackmail attempt had a paradoxical effect. Banking on the public's anger at a single woman in an Islamic country having sex, they had miscalculated. The scandal increased Ismayilova's profile, making her work more widely known. Family, friends, and even Azerbaijan's Islamic Party rallied to her defense. But behind Ismayilova's public veneer of resolve, the personal cost was steep. The relationship with her boyfriend ended. She wondered whether he had been complicit in the filming. The loss of trust impeded new relationships. When she found out that the cameras in her apartment had been installed in her bathroom, too, her body shut down. "I had to smile in public," she divulged. "I had to continue working. But I was physically broken."

In the depths of despair, she recalls a female student she was mentoring at the time telling her to stop whining and push on with her investigations. "That woman saved my life," Ismayilova said. She went on to publish the findings from four major investigations that year, the most productive of her career.

New tactics were employed to silence her. She was arrested on trumped-up charges of harassing a colleague but released when the government's case collapsed. She was then convicted of evading taxes, another bogus charge, and given a seven and a half–

year jail sentence. After eighteen months in prison, her sentence was commuted to two years and three months, with five years of probation. Online bullying from government trolls continues.

Ismayilova's resilience is remarkable. She told me that she is driven by "the people's right to know." In her pursuit of the truth, she is therefore sustaining one of the cornerstones of civil society: the right of citizens to hold their leaders accountable. But there are other forces, subtler and less obvious, at play.

Her guilt in relation to Huseynov's murder and her shame when the *Washington Post* came calling on the Dubai property scandal are telling, for shame and guilt are the primary emotions associated with moral injury. This concept refers to damage done to one's conscience or moral compass by perpetrating, witnessing, or failing to prevent acts that transgress one's own beliefs, values, or ethical codes of conduct.* When we place this definition alongside Ismayilova's meticulous exposé of her government's sleaze, the fit is immediately apparent. Such gross corruption is outrageous—we are morally affronted by it. However, only a select few are prepared to do something about it. Murder, blackmail, character assassination, and financial ruin may silence the majority, but not Ismayilova.

When I asked whether she worried about the risks associated with her reporting, she replied: "You get a gut feeling before publication that something bad might happen, but your first thought is to get it out there. Because if you do not publish, you feel very bad about it. You feel like you gave up; you were scared. This is not a good feeling to live with. It's actually easier to spit it out."

There you have it: the blackmail, public shaming, jail time, the pain of it all, preferable to keeping quiet. Ismayilova's father dared speak out against corrup-

---

* Syracuse University. "What is moral injury?" *The What Is Moral Injury Project.* Accessed: 2023. https://moralinjuryproject.syr.edu/about-moral-injury/

Ismayilova's laptop and indispensable multiple cellphones.

tion in Heydar Aliyev's government. Her mother was a dissident in the days of the Soviet Union. Their daughter has gone many steps further in her pursuit of the truth and accountability. In doing so, she has received some notable honors, including a Right Livelihood Award, known as the Alternative Nobel Prize.

Affirming as awards may be, they cannot explain what set Khadija Ismayilova on her career trajectory. An inquiring mind got her started, but it is an unshakeable moral compass that has kept her at it despite everything thrown at her. Staying true to one's ethical code can lead to prison in Ilham Aliyev's Azerbaijan, and many other places in this world. But there is a rare, precious upside, too. "I feel accomplished," Ismayilova said. "Despite everything, I feel happy."

Chin'ono in his home office. Harare, Zimbabwe.

Hopewell Rugoho-Chin'ono

The Zimbabwean journalist Hopewell Rugoho-Chin'ono was born in 1971 when his country was still known as Rhodesia. The Bush War had begun seven years back, pitting Black liberation movements against the old while colonial regime lead by Prime Minister Ian Smith. It was a time of escalating violence and great uncertainty.

Perhaps this is the reason why Chin'ono's parents named their son Hopewell. There is a rich tradition surrounding African names, and in Zimbabwe, in particular, parental choice may be influenced by the mood or circumstances of family at the time of birth.

The war had a profound influence on Chin'ono's childhood. His father, while a supporter of the liberation struggle, worked as a civil servant. Being employed by the minority white government meant he was incorrectly viewed by insurgents as a sellout. There were threats to kill him, which meant the family had to keep moving to keep him safe. Chin'ono attended four different schools in three years. There were periods of separation from his father.

Other pressures were foisted on the child by circumstances beyond the family's control. He was the youngest of five children, and the age gap was such that his siblings had already left home during his childhood. This left him alone with his mother, who had bipolar disorder. When she became unwell, the child became the parent, and when psychosis and mania made the situation impossible to manage, it fell to him to have his mother hospitalized. This raw exposure to mental illness left its mark. He would return to the subject matter as an adult in his work.

Above: *Chin'ono greets traders in a local market.*

Zimbabwe became independent in 1980, and the Bush war ended after fifteen years of conflict, leaving an estimated twenty thousand dead. In a country of only seven million people, the casualty rate was equivalent to a million dead Americans. Peace brought some stability to Chin'ono's family, but it was also a time for revenge and retribution in Zimbabwe.

President Robert Mugabe's Zimbabwe African National Union-Patriotic Front (ZANU-PF) party had won a landslide victory, and in a national address to the nation after taking power, the president, who had spent eleven years as a political prisoner, spoke generously of reconciliation: "If you were my enemy, you are now my friend. If you hated me, you cannot avoid the love that binds me to you now."

Away from the high-flown rhetoric, the reality on the ground was very different. Mission schools were the bedrock of black education in Zimbabwe. Chin'ono attended one of them, run by the United Methodist Church and funded by the Americans. The headmaster, a bishop, had contested the election in opposition to ZANU-PF. As payback, he and his clerics were booted out and control of the school handed over to party loyalists.

Chin'ono's father was distressed by the damage done to the country's education system. He prized learning, and rather than accept lower standards and the injustice of these summary dismissals, sent his son to another school. "I have no money to leave you," Chin'ono recalls his father telling him, "but you will have an education and this can take you as far as you want." His words proved prophetic.

As a teenager, Chin'ono won an English competition sponsored by the magazine *Prize Beat*. This led to him being offered his own column with the magazine and a remarkably free hand. "Write anything you want," he remembers being told. "Let the readers know how you perceive things." It says much for a precocious talent that this offer was made to a schoolboy. More kudos quickly followed. When the reggae star Dennis Brown visited Zimbabwe, Chin'ono was sent to interview him. The edition sold out. More interviews flowed his way. As Chin'ono likes to say, he became a journalist by chance, not design.

After completing high school, Chin'ono studied journalism at the Zimbabwe Institute of Mass Communications. He graduated in 1993 and left for London, his destination influenced by his admiration for the British Broadcasting Corporation, which he has listened to with his father while growing up. A master's degree in journalism from City University was followed by an internship at the BBC World Service in London.

Trouble back in Zimbabwe was casting a long shadow, and it fell on the BBC, too. Land reform was underway, white-owned farms were being expropriated, often violently, and international correspondents covering the story had been expelled from the country. Chin'ono proposed to the BBC that he be sent to report on the situation. As a citizen, he could get back into Zimbabwe. In theory, the plan looked good and the BBC agreed, but it all came to nothing when the Zimbabwean government refused to register him as a BBC journalist and insisted that he seek accreditation through a local government-controlled entity. Chin'ono balked at this muzzle. While waiting for the dispute to resolve, he learned that he had won a British government Chevening Scholarship designed to attract outstanding emerging leaders from all over the world.

Back in London, he completed a second master's degree, this time in documentary practice at Brunel University, and made his first film. *Pain in My Heart* is a twenty-six-minute documentary that focused on the HIV-AIDS epidemic in Zimbabwe and the inequalities in access to health care that determined who lived and died. The film was a critical success and won many awards for Chin'ono, including CNN's African Journalist of the Year. It opened the door to TV broadcasting for him and signaled his emergence as a journalist using his craft to highlight social causes and injustice.

After making his documentary, Chin'ono set up his own television production house and began working for ITV

Chin'ono consults with his lawyer, Doug Coltart, at the Magistrate's Court, Harare, Zimbabwe.

while based in Zimbabwe. From there, it was on to Boston and a Nieman Fellowship at Harvard University for a year before returning to ITV. In time, he would begin writing for the *New York Times*, covering the floundering social situation in Zimbabwe. Along the way, there were other well-received documentaries that he directed and produced, all relating to human rights and social justice issues.

In 2016, Chin'ono began devoting himself full-time to documentary making with a film called *State of Mind*. It was a story painfully close to home, for it exposed the plight of the mentally ill in Zimbabwe, a topic that he knew all too well from his childhood. He was four years old when his mother's bipolar disorder first manifested. She had lived her life in and out of psychiatric wards. Her illness, typically characterized by dramatic relapses followed by remissions, was one of the defining aspects of his childhood. Alone with his emotionally fragile mother, Chin'ono recalls that the "abnormal became the normal" for him, a poignant description of what his life was like at the time.

The stigma of mental illness in Zimbabwe was so powerful, families hid unwell relatives who they believed were possessed by demons. Not so for Chin'ono's father. He sat his young son down and told him all about mental illness and what to expect with his mother, preparing him for the inevitable breakdowns that would occur and which he would have to manage in his father's absence. It was an extraordinary strategy, indicative of an enlightened attitude and a desperate necessity.

In revisiting the subject of mental illness forty years on from his childhood experiences, Chin'ono lifted the lid on the anguish that accompanied people stigmatized and left untreated. His film also became a metaphor for the failed Zimbabwe state. With no prospect of work, young men were taking solace in drugs that triggered psychosis. What followed was admission to mental institutions shelled out by corruption, which meant there was no money for the medications essential for treatment.

Chin'ono's documentaries on taboo subjects in Zimbabwe like AIDS and mental illness brought attention to lives lived in the shadows. In doing so, he kept faith with a guiding principle that defined his journalism, the need to articulate social issues. As he sees it, broadcasters typically focus on hard politics when reporting the news. To him, it is more informative to explain politics by looking at how people live their lives. "A nation should not be judged by how it treats its highest citizens, but its lowest ones," declared Nelson Mandela. Using this as a moral yardstick, Chin'ono's work was a damning indictment of Zimbabwe's failure to address pressing social concerns.

Six months after *State of Mind* was released, a coup toppled President Mugabe. His successor, President Emmerson Mnangagwa, promised to clean shop and address rampant corruption. Chin'ono was approached by the Minister of Information, Monica Mutsvangwa, with a request to help rehabilitate the Zimbabwe Broadcasting Corporation. The country's only television station had become "a propaganda outfit for the government," Chin'ono recalls. Western governments were prepared to help financially. When Chin'ono, fearing more corruption, recommended that the World Bank manage the donations, the government pushed back and plans for reform fell through. "They thought they were going to get a blank check," he told me.

It was soon clear to Chin'ono that the Mnangagwa regime was nothing more than old wine in new bottles, if not worse. Corruption remained rampant. The economy was in ruins. A direct clash between the him and the authorities was just a matter of time. The COVID-19 pandemic was the tipping point. Chin'ono turned to social media to reveal that money was being looted from public funds earmarked for personal protective equipment. He was charged with incitement to cause public violence and spent forty-five days in prison. The Zimbabwean Health Minister Dr. Obadiah Moyo was subsequently fired in relation to the scandal and the charges against Chin'ono dismissed by the High Court.

Two further arrests followed. In one of these, he was charged under a law that was defunct. In the other, the charge was obstruction of justice in relation to a story he broke about the president's niece about to get bail unopposed in relation to charges of smuggling six kilograms of gold to Dubai. In total, he has spent eighty-five days in jail in appalling conditions, eating slop, sleeping on the floor, without access to running water or toilet paper, the latter forcing inmates to tear pages from the Bible, an embarrassing and humiliating substitute. And while confined, he rubbed shoulders during a pandemic with hundreds of prisoners who were not wearing masks because there were none as a result of the broken public healthcare system.

For fifteen years, Chin'ono has been intensely engaged in covering the turmoil and despair that has engulfed his country. In doing so, he has also faced incessant online harassment. There have been occasions he has feared for his life, tweeting about his concerns to his followers while stating that he would not be intimidated. Yet his motivation to continue his work remains strong. In trying to understand the origins of where this drive comes from, insights can be gleaned from his childhood and the parental influences that shaped him. His father may have been a civil servant in a white minority government, but he refused to be subjugated by his colonial-era employers. Chin'ono remembers hearing, as a child, District Commissioner David Williams threatening to have his father killed, a threat that was not carried out, Chin'ono believes, only because Williams died in a landmine incident soon thereafter. Chino'ono also recollects his mother telling him that big crowds can make wrong decisions. If you stand alone, knowing what you do is right is what matters, she advised him.

If his parents, as role models, set the moral tone of his life, it was the collapse of civil society in Zimbabwe that put these core beliefs to the test. To stay or leave? To speak up or stay quiet? That Chin'ono remained and "started making noise" links his journalism to social activism even though the activist label does not sit easily with him, for he views himself as an accidental witness to life in Zimbabwe. The news found him, he reminded me. As he ruefully observed, there are no uplifting stories in Zimbabwe as there are in functioning democracies, of hospitals being built or great agricultural projects providing food for the masses. Instead, people complain endlessly about the destroyed economy and crippling corruption, and because journalists report on life around them, these complaints become the topics of his stories. He simply reports what he sees and hears.

This watered-down explanation is, however, only part of the equation, as Chin'ono knows full well. "All the news that's fit to print" trumpets the *New York Times*'s famous motto. Chin'ono once worked for this paper, and applying their core tenet of good journalism to his country has led to his incarceration and harassment. In a revealing interview with the Reuters Institute for the Study of Journalism, he spoke of how his arrest had the effect of emboldening, not intimidating him. "I don't care if they kill me today. I only care about how I'm going to be remembered."

This reference to his legacy seems key to me in understanding the source of his motivation. Not to fear death takes physical courage, but to be remembered favorably for what you stood for demands moral courage. Hopewell Chin'ono does not want to be known as the man who kept quiet. "There is a huge impact on society if people like myself are silenced by a corrupt regime," he told me.

Silence is a theme he circles back to repeatedly and from many different angles. "I enable corruption by keeping quiet," he believes. Addressing me directly he notes that "saying something that puts me in jail helps because you and I would not be having this conversation if I had kept quiet." Even mulling over whether to speak out is seen as abrogating a duty. "The moment we start debating whether to expose something, we are failing as journalists." And most importantly, the practical benefits of holding a corrupt government accountable for its sins are emphasized. "If I had not exposed looting, the plundering of national resources, a lot more people would have died from Covid."

Chin'ono is the recipient of multiple journalism awards.

What unites all these variations on a theme of speaking out, are the emotions associated with acts of omission when confronted by egregious behavior. "I see myself as someone with a global voice and I would be ashamed to have failed to use that global voice when you are around people who have no voice at all," Chin'ono explained. "I would feel so guilty if I did not do this. When I go to the United Nations and am asked to talk about myself, I prefer to talk about my people, how they have suffered. I feel a sense of guilt in talking about myself."

This most articulate of people could not spell it out more clearly when he says: "I don't want to be remembered as the person who did nothing. Guilt and shame have always been central to the things that I do." In this revelation, we see the consequences of moral injury writ large, the primary emotions of the condition centerstage alongside an act of omission And the remedy for it is the moral courage that compels Chin'ono to speak out even if that means arrest or death. The shame that comes with silence is more painful than the worst punishment a punitive government can inflict on him.

Chin'ono's outspoken condemnation of what is wrong in Zimbabwe today is solace to his downtrodden fellow citizens. He makes sure they are heard and in doing so instills hope of better days that perhaps await. In naming their youngest child Hopewell, Chin'ono's parents were expressing a wish for his future. They could not have known how prescient their choice would prove to be.

Above and right: *Holcová. Prague, Czech Republic.*

CZECH REPUBLIC AND SLOVAKIA

Pavla Holcová

Pavla Holcová always wanted to be a journalist. As a journalism student, she had hopes of becoming a war reporter, attracted by what she saw as the adrenaline rush that came with this work. Her family background and upbringing in Czechoslovakia certainly did not lack for moments of great historical drama and excitement. A great grandfather, Jiri Hejda, who opposed the Communist revolution in 1948, had been sentenced to death, subsequently commuted to twenty-five years in jail, in an infamous political trial that saw the execution of politician Milada Horáková on fabricated charges of treason. Standout memories from her childhood include three-month hiking trips across parts of Europe and America with her "hippie" mother and siblings, living rough, at times

traversing regions that were dangerous, like cartel-infiltrated northern Mexico—experiences she recalls as both exhilarating and exhausting.

Her first journalism job, however, was the very antithesis of what she thought her career would be: a nightshift, copying and rewriting news provided by the agencies. She lasted eight months before resigning. By now, she was a young mother. War zones were no longer an option, but the desire for work that eschewed the mundane and routine remained. She joined an NGO, People in Need, tasked with supporting independent journalism in Cuba. At the time, Cuban journalism followed one of two tracks, she recalled. The pro-government press blamed the United States for everything while dissenters in turn blamed the government. Her job was to create publications that replaced biased polemics with fact-based reportage, no easy task in a totalitarian state. She ran her program from an office in Prague but spent two months a year in Cuba. And it was there that she ended up in prison, an event that changed the course of her life.

The year was 2007, and Holcová had traveled to Cuba with Paul Radu, cofounder of the Organized Crime and Corruption Reporting Project (OCCRP). One evening, she and Radu went to a bar reserved for foreigners where they struck up a conversation with a man who, after he became drunk, divulged that he was bringing military parts into Cuba under cover of a business registered in Spain that purportedly traded in agricultural equipment. In retrospect, they should have paid more attention to the man's date: a stone-cold sober young Cuban woman. At four o'clock the following morning, the police knocked on their hotel door and took them into custody.

As Holcová wryly noted, you get to know someone quite well after being forced to spend five days together in a cell-like room with a single exposed toilet. Looking back on her detention, she sees it as a critical moment in her career, the enforced proximity with Radu affording her the opportunity to become better acquainted with his work at OCCRP. In Havana, under lock and key in Fidel Castro's police state, the idea of becoming an investigative journalist first came to her.

On her return to the Czech Republic, Holcová did not immediately leave her job with People in Need. While her team was expelled from Cuba, she was allowed to return after a year. She kept at it for a number of years, working assiduously to boost fact-based journalism, but it was apparent to her that nothing was really changing in Cuba. And so in 2013, inspired by Radu's work, Holcová founded the Czech Centre for Investigative Journalism.

The OCCRP working model required cross-border cooperation. Links had been established across the Balkans, Eastern Europe, the Caucasus, Central Asia, and Central America to probe and expose global crime syndicates. Holcová was aware that the "black hole" in this investigative web was the Czech Republic. Nobody in her country was doing this kind of work. She resolved to plug the gap.

The Czech Centre for Investigative Journalism had a grand-sounding name, but no money or resources or indeed journalist sources within the country. Holcová might have had Radu's enthusiastic virtual backing, but to begin with, she was quite alone, a one-person organization. She supported herself financially by taking a job at an IT company, working a full-time day job with programmers and coders. Her night job was investigative journalism. She was also a wife and mother.

She started collaborating with colleagues at OCCRP and the International Consortium of Investigative Journalists (ICIJ). Through the ICIJ, she got access to the Panama Papers, 11.5 million leaked legal and financial documents exposing a system that facilitated a vast network of crime and corruption sheltering incognito, until then in offshore companies. Her first big story came out of a collaboration with Azerbaijani journalist Khadija Ismayilova, in which they revealed the illicit investments in the Czech Republic of the Azerbaijani ruling family headed by President Ilham Aliyev. The story had little impact in Prague but contributed to Ismayilova's imprisonment in Azerbaijan.

Holcová then turned her attention to revealing illicit Russian property deals in the Czech Republic. She was learning on the job, reliant on students for assistance as she could not as yet afford to hire staff. When OCCRP bought a story, she got paid. In 2016, she quit her IT position to focus full time on investigative work. Together with Macedonian journalist Saska Cvetkovska, she exposed the illegal, secret investments of Macedonia's chief of secret police, Sašo Mijalkov, leading to his resignation and a domino effect that brought down the Macedonian government three years later. That a fledgling Czech organization with such limited resources could have such a dramatic impact, ending fifteen years of rule from corrupt, seemingly "untouchable politicians baked in their positions," as Holcová described them, sent a powerful message not only to organized crime, but also to her journalist colleagues in the Czech Republic who had viewed the efforts of a neophyte with condescension.

The release of the Pandora Papers in 2021, a trove of documents that exceeded the Panama papers in size, scope, and scale, provided fresh evidence of crime, corruption, and the malfeasance of politicians. By now, the Czech Centre for Investigative Journalism had eleven full-time employees. With access to the Pandora Papers, Holcová revealed that Czech Prime Minister Andrej Babis, known to his detractors as the "Czech Trump" and long tainted by the whiff of financial impropriety, had secretly moved 22 million dollars through offshore companies to buy a property on the French Riviera.

The news of the financial scandal broke just before an election. The prime minister accused Holcová of manipulating the facts. She was banned from attending his press conferences. Video footage emerged showing his bodyguards pushing her away from his presser. The rough handing of Holcová became part of the story. Andrej Babis and his ANO party lost the election.

There is a continuum of danger faced by frontline and investigative journalists. As they inch upward along this spectrum of risk in pursuit of the story, they come closer to death. In war zones, death for some may arrive randomly, a life ended by the smallest of details. General MacArthur, no stranger to the subject, knew this only too well: "In war, you win or lose, live or die and the difference is just an eyelash."

To the investigative journalist, however, death may visit differently. It is seldom, if ever, a chance event. Here, there is clarity of purpose, even as the perpetrators take refuge in shadows, obfuscation, and increasingly, fake news. This is the fate that befell twenty-seven-year-old Slovak journalist Ján Kuciak. That his twenty-seven-year old fiancée, Martina Kusnirova, was murdered with him is readily explainable, too, by the harsh constructs that define a contract killing: witnesses can talk.

Holcová in the yard of the Czech Center for Investigative Journalism. So strong is her commitment to her profession, she views her job as part of her personality.

At the time of his murder, Kuciak was working with Holcová on a story exposing corruption in the highest echelons of the Slovak government. She recalls with eidetic clarity the moment she learned of her colleague's death. It was eight o'clock on a Monday morning when she received a phone call from Marek Vogovič, Kuciak's editor at *Aktuality*. "You should sit down," he told her, "because a terrible tragedy has happened."

Holcová had first met Kuciak five years earlier when he was still a student. Together, they had released a story detailing how a Swedish company had broken the law by employing Slovak workers in substandard working conditions. She recalls that Kuciak had a fine, analytical mind and was able to unravel and make sense of complex financial documents. This made him a valuable partner when it came to exposing byzantine money laundering schemes. Holcová also considered him as a friend.

Their last investigation began when Kuciak called her with news that the Slovak prime minster, Robert Fico, had hired a new assistant, Maria Toskova, whose slim résumé included beauty pageant contestant, posing topless in a girlie magazine, and according to the Slovak Business Registry, former business partner of one Antonio Vadalà, a mafioso from the notorious 'Ndrangheta family in Calabria, Italy. Nuggets like these deserved further scrutiny. Over the course of eighteen months, the two journalists unearthed evidence linking the Italian Mafia to SMER, Slovakia's ruling party. Kuciak and his fiancée were murdered before the full story could be released.

In the immediate aftermath of the murder, Czech police, acting on advice from their Slovakian colleagues, moved quickly to protect Holcová and her family. They were taken to an undisclosed destination deep in a forest and given round-the-clock protection. She did not have access to a phone. She had to turn off the TV because it was full of news of the double murder. OCCRP deemed it essential to her safety that the story she and Kuciak had been working on be released quickly. Two days after the killings, the story broke.

The ramifications were profound. Huge protests roiled Slovakia. Within a month, Prime Minister Fico and his cabinet resigned. The tentacles of corruption were shown to extend to the upper echelons of Slovakia's judiciary and law enforcement agencies, prompting multiple high-profile resignations of judges and the suicide of a police chief in jail awaiting trial.

The twin killings left Kuciak's and Kusnirova's parents bereft and Holcová in shock. Following two weeks in seclusion, she returned to Prague. Police protection continued for the next six months. She wore a chip that tracked her movements. "Part of my brain was on fire, the other half frozen," she told me. By nature a happy person, she could no longer experience joy. As she went through the autopsy reports and looked at photographs of the murder scene, she felt all her emotions but one shutting down. Only guilt remained, irrational she knew, but impervious to reason. Individuals become fixated to their moments of trauma, observed Sigmund Freud.

Looking back at events, Holcová wondered if she, the more experienced of the two journalists, could have done things differently to avert the tragedy. As an investigative journalist, she was being told to be careful so often the warnings had become almost pro forma, their perfunctory quality losing the power to instill alarm. "You have a life to live," she explained, "you cannot be afraid all the time." Under these circumstances, habituation is inevitable. A person cannot live in a constant state of anticipatory anxiety. When a threat is replaced by action, no amount of insight softens the blow.

In time, Holcová would be diagnosed with PTSD. Compounding her trauma was a concerted campaign of online harassment from the supporters of Prime Minister Fico, who blamed her for his fall. She was threatened with rape. "Be careful crossing the street," she was warned. "There is boiling water for every pig, even for someone like you," she was told ominously.

Undeterred by threats and grief, Holcová continued her work. She speaks poignantly of visiting the murder scene one

Despite grave personal risks in exposing crime, Holcová's resolve is clear: "Doing nothing is not an option."

year later accompanied by Kuciak's mother and father and Kusnirova's mother. Blood stains were still visible on the floor. Her anxiety about how the parents would receive her dissolved in the face of their love and solicitous concern for her well-being.

By then, it was known that the mafia was not behind the murders. Suspicion fell on Marian Kocner, a local businessman connected to the ruling party. Kuciak had written extensively about Kocner's questionable financial dealings, arousing the ire of the vindictive, choleric oligarch. Three locals, Miroslav Marcek, Tomas Szabo and Zoltan Andrusko, were convicted of the killings, and the latter implicated Kocner as the instigator. Kocner was charged with the murder and acquitted, only for the acquittal to be overturned. He is to be retried. Meanwhile, he waits in jail, having in the interim received a nineteen-year sentence for fraud in a case that arose from Kuciak's reporting.

In less than a decade since Holcová decided to found the Czech Centre for Investigative Journalism, there have been some notable successes. She has received prestigious awards. But the price has been high. A close colleague has been murdered. Her marriage has ended, in part because of the strains that come with work that brings danger into the home. I asked her if it had all been worthwhile when we met during her visit to Toronto for the premiere of her documentary, *The Killing of a Journalist*.

By way of an answer, she told me of a question she had asked herself as a young adult when she read books of her country's repressive communist past. "Would I have been the one to join the opposition, the dissenters, even if it meant being sent to jail, or having my children threatened? Would I have been the strong one fighting for the values I believed in? Or would I have failed. Would I have been part of the silent majority? And I had no answer, but I was afraid I would have failed."

In this revealing passage, we see a core feature that motivates Pavla Holcová today. Investigative journalism has given her the means to assuage a self-doubt tethered to the potential for moral injury. When she looks at the risks she now faces in her work, she is able to say with conviction and clarity: "Doing nothing is not an option." In the twenty-first century, her questions wrapped in an implicit challenge to herself no longer relate to opposing the diktats of Soviet masters, but rather to where she stands on corruption and state capture and the power of money undermining fairness, decency, and the rule of law.

An understanding of what moral injury is and how it can profoundly influence behavior reveals a thread that links generations of Holcová's family. Doing nothing, an act of omission, in the face of morally egregious behavior was not an option for her great-grandfather seventy-five years ago. The same holds true for his granddaughter today. The imperative to act and persevere rather than look away, knowing full well the consequences that can follow, speaks to an unwavering moral courage.

The lure of investigative journalism has proved irresistible to Holcová. Not only does it offer work in tune with a finely set moral compass, it also connects her to colleagues with a similar mindset. There is a deep camaraderie between investigative journalists, the intensity of their bonds forged by high stakes laced with risk and ever-present danger that define the nature of their work. "This job is part of my personality," she told me. "If I gave it up, I would be giving up a part of myself."

Dojčinović stands of the roof of his office building. Belgrade, Serbia.

Stevan Dojčinović

For the past fifteen years, Serbian investigative journalist Stevan Dojčinović has worked relentlessly to expose corruption, money laundering and government links to crime syndicates at home and in the Balkans. As a result, thirty-eight-year-old Dojčinović has been ruthlessly targeted by a coterie of gangsters, crooked politicians, and villainous government officials. Such is the intensity of threat, slander, and harassment directed at him that almost half his life has been spent under siege, fending off a deluge of fake news designed to break his spirit and silence his voice.

Corruption in the Balkans extends into the upper echelons of government, and Dojčinović's exposés have made him some formidable enemies. Some examples: The former mayor of Belgrade, Sinisa

Mali—now Serbia's minister of finance—has a modest salary, yet somehow has control over forty-five bank accounts and reportedly was involved in the purchase of twenty-four apartments on Bulgaria's Black Sea coast. Indicted cocaine smuggler Darko Saric has strong business ties with Prva Banka, a bank owned by the family of Montenegro's prime minister, Milo Djukanovic. "Follow the money," goes the catchphrase, if you want to unearth corruption. Balkan politics is the exemplar of this sound advice.

And then there is Serbia's minister of health, Dr. Zlatibor Lončar, who has a long-standing association with Peter Panic, a one-eyed mobster connected to the Zemun Clan, one of Serbia's most powerful mafia groups. Before entering

Above: Dojčinović holds a scanner to detect cameras used for surveillance of him and fellow journalists.

politics, Lončar was a practicing physician who provided Panic, who was facing assault charges, with suspect medical reports that helped the mobster delay—and in one case circumvent—the course of justice.

In 1985, the year of Dojčinović's birth, Serbia was still part of Yugoslavia. His father was an engineer, his mother an economist, and in time his younger brother would become a lawyer. When the Balkan civil wars started six years later, the family was living in Krusevac, 200 kilometers from the capital, Belgrade. The city was spared the fighting but not the economic hardships that came with international embargoes and sanctions. These were "the nightmare years," Dojčinović says, during which Yugoslavia tore itself apart. Like Many Serbian families, the Dojčinoviés suffered financially. Childhood holidays to the beaches of Greece stopped. Crime, however, never skipped a beat. Even as a schoolboy, young Stevan was aware of its ubiquitous presence. "You could feel it," he recalled. A number of people were murdered at the local pub, 200 meters down the road from his home.

There was even a tacit playground hierarchy in place. Everyone knew they better be nice to the "top kid"—the one who had a big brother with links to organized crime.

Growing up in a repressive socialist state, rife with crime and buffeted by the remnants of ruinous civil war, left Dojčinović feeling disillusioned. His form of dissent against the state of affairs was to join a protest movement. He became a punk, the archetype of teen rebellion and alienation. Recognizing that he lacked musical talent, but determined to contribute to the movement, he started a punk magazine, LBVKBVRDa, with responsibility not only for editorial content, but also sales and distribution throughout the Balkans. It was around the same time that he revealed an additional propensity for risk-taking by embracing extreme urban bike riding. The day before the terrorist attacks of 9/11, one of his bike stunts went horribly wrong. Months in hospital followed, with multiple surgeries to repair a shattered jaw—for a year thereafter, all his meals were taken through a straw.

Dojčinović is featured and attacked in the pro-government tabloid newspaper, The Informer.

Dojčinović went on to study political science at the University of Belgrade. His course work included journalism classes that left him disillusioned. He did not want to learn the profession from books. It was during this period of uncertainty, adrift in his career choice, that he began reading *The Assassination of Zoran*, Milo Vasic's book about the murder of Serbian prime minister Zoran Dindić, killed by a sniper's bullet in 2003. Vasic was an investigative journalist who founded the independent Serbian weekly *Vreme* in 1990, at the height of Serbian strongman Slobodan Milošević's rule. His journalism exposed the shadowy connections between organized crime, political leaders, and the intelligence services in Serbia and the Balkans. His masterful account of the assassination was a continuation of this theme, revealing how organized crime was behind the targeted killing of Serbia's progressive, democratic leader.

"Milo Vasic's book transformed my life," Dojčinović says, noting that it opened his eyes to the power of investigative journalism. There it was, tens of thousands of documents meticulously researched and laid out, like the work of a prosecutor, all wrapped up in beautifully clear prose that gripped your attention and held it even though one knew the outcome before starting to read. Dojčinović saw how investigative journalism would give him the means to push back against a corrupt regime—just the way his earlier punk phase had done, but this time with a formal career that went beyond mere protest by holding out the promise of positive change as well. This was the kind of journalism a world removed from the dry, passionless approach foisted on him at university. And moreover, to a young man who had delighted in extreme sports, it came with a frisson of risk and excitement, too. Stevan Dojčinović had found his *métier*.

Before he could begin working as an investigative journalist, Dojčinović needed training. He looked for this outside the university, and for a few months worked for the public broadcaster RTS but did not find the experience rewarding. In 2007, he attended a training seminar given by Paul

Radu, the cofounder of the Organized Crime and Corruption Reporting Project (OCCRP). With Radu's training and mentoring, Dojčinović became an investigative journalist, and in 2008, he began working for OCCRP.

Seven years later, he founded KRIK, an organization with the same mandate as OCCRP, but publishing in Serbian instead of English. Based in Belgrade, he learned that crime on a grand scale did not respect a nation's borders, and that it required a multinational team to reveal its many tentacles. In one of Dojčinović's first big exposés, he worked alongside colleagues in Serbia, Romania, Bulgaria, and Bosnia to show how criminals had infiltrated the lucrative casino market.

Another lesson was that investigating a major crime network could take a long time. In 2010, Dojčinović began looking into the Saric cartel, Europe's largest network of cocaine dealers. Four years of intense, dangerous, adrenaline-soaked work led to the exposure of the crimes of gang leader Darko Saric, leading henchman Rodol-jub Radulović (a.k.a. "Banana"), and chief financier Zoran Copic.

Dojčinović's tireless efforts to expose crime and corruption in Serbia has made his life a "nightmare" at times—a descriptor he uses repeatedly when speaking to the adversity he now faces. While organized crime killed prime minister Zoran Dindić in 2003, Dojčinović does not believe that members of the political elite who remain hand-in-glove with the criminals will resort once more to assassination to silence him. As he wryly noted, killing journalists or incarcerating them would not improve the chances of Serbia's long-held desire to join the European Union. Instead, the method of attack now is a different form of assassination—one that targets his character. The government controls the media. They have law enforcement in their back pocket. They shamelessly exploit the reach and power of the internet. They use all three prongs relentlessly, which gives them a vast array of powers to be used nefariously and with impunity.

Impugning Dojčinović's character fol-

Dojčinović in Belgrade, Serbia. He describes his life as a "nightmare" at times given the decades of harassment he has endured.

lows a stereotypical playbook. He has been accused of being a CIA agent. He has been linked to S&M sex clubs. He is constantly being sued. There are currently ten cases open against him. To date, he has escaped the bogus tax audit, a favored intimidation ploy that's like catnip to repressive regimes. His media colleagues have not been so fortunate. The apartment of a KRIK employee has been broken into. Once again, the vandalism follows a familiar script. The place is turned upside down, the contents trashed, but nothing is ever stolen. The message behind the mess is clear: You have no privacy, no security, not even your home is safe. Reporting the break-in to the police is pointless. There is no avenue to seek redress.

The harassment of journalists started in earnest when the Serbian Progressive Party under President Tomislac Nikolić took power in 2012. Nikolić had been deputy prime minister during the rule of Slobodan Milošević, who had died six years earlier in prison in the Hague, where he was being tried for war crimes by the International Criminal Tribunal. Old habits die hard. An even more disturbing recent development is a concerted government attempt to connect Dojčinović and KRIK to organized crime. This smear not only hinders Dojčinović's work—his exposés often depend on his sources within organized crime and the police—it also comes with grave perils for him. Being pinned to a particular crime group in the cutthroat Balkan underworld runs the risk of making him the target of rival groups. When the dangers became too acute in 2020, he had to flee Serbia for a month.

There is no break in this orchestrated persecution. Dojčinović has no downtime. Rare attempts at a short vacation are invariably upended by scurrilous new accusations. "You can't sit at the beach sipping a cocktail and put off responding for five days until your holiday is over," he says. So it goes—the days running into weeks, months, and years of intimidation designed to wear him down, crushing him under the sheer weight of it all. And the harassment doesn't end there. Segments of the public are inflamed by government manipulation, and Dojčinović receives death threats and a lot of hate mail. No wonder, then, that he feels weary—"I am like a fifty-year-old man," he says—his fatigue hard to shake. And all the while, assailed by these distractions, at times emotionally spent, he still has to keep on working.

So what has kept Dojčinović in Serbia, continuing to unearth crime and corruption? The answer may be found in the epiphany he experienced when he began reading Milo Vasic's book—that with investigative journalism, one could "do a good thing to counteract a bad thing." Couched in terms like these, of good versus bad, his efforts take on a moral imperative. The ethically egregious behavior of politicians in cahoots with gangsters—an association that reached its malign apotheosis with the murder of a democratically elected, reform-minded prime minister—simply cannot be accepted. Journalism gave him the means to fight back. Doing nothing—an act of omission when seen within the context of moral injury—has never been an option, even if it means placing himself in

the crosshairs of a government that works ceaselessly to destroy his credibility.

Given the forces arrayed against him, there is a constant tension in Dojčinović's life. Work both destroys his life and rewards it. Revealing corruption motivates yet stresses him. The thought of living elsewhere is attractive yet troubling—the advantages of a more tranquil life in a different country, longed-for during periods of intense anxiety, competing with worries about the boredom and lack of purpose to his life that could come with walking away from OCCRP and KRIK. All of this makes for a roller-coaster experience. "When you finish a story, you have this nice feeling—it's the perfect day. [But] tomorrow the nightmare starts."

Dojčinović is clear-eyed about what he can achieve. He recognizes that exposing corruption among the political elite in Serbia will not have the same immediate impact as in a country like Canada, for example, where politicians are held more accountable. But he has an eye on the future. He believes preserving a historical record of

Dojčinović has his eye on the future and the importance of preserving a historical record of crimes and misdemeanors.

crimes and misdemeanors—something no one else is doing in Serbia—is important. He sees investigative journalists fulfilling an essential civic function, keeping their fellow citizens informed of what is happening in their own country. And ultimately, there will be a reckoning. "We are touching the untouchables," he points out. Accountability will not be denied.

It would be remiss to conclude that the challenges Dojčinović and his colleagues face are specific to the Balkans, notwithstanding the region's long history of political instability. In an address to the International Centre for Journalists, which honored him with their Knight Award in 2019, he explained how a toxic imbroglio of crime and corruption, undercutting and weakening the rule of law, was attractive to autocrats, extremists, and ultranationalists the world over. It gave them a manual on how to subvert and take over a democracy. Each step along this slippery road was spelled out—and it all begins with undermining the media, using it to manipulate and distract people, and when necessary, to destroy the activists, judiciary, and credible journalists who get in the way.

Placing Dojčinović's work in this broader context, where the stakes are so high, gives us a more complete appreciation of what he is up against. At the same time, it also shines a bright light on his tenacity in the face of adversity and a refusal to buckle under intense pressure—the very embodiments of a moral courage that keeps him going.

Kumwenda looking out her office window at Crown TV. Lusaka, Zambia.

Mwape Kumwenda

It was simply a matter of timing that led Mwape Kumwenda into journalism rather than law, her initial choice. She saw both careers giving her the bully pulpit to fight for social justice. But having just completed secondary school, she would have to wait six months before applying to law school. There was no such delay with journalism. Her impatience at wanting to begin advocating for the downtrodden of society was such that she switched career track with alacrity and without regret.

What is striking about Kumwenda's career path is that she knew what she wanted to achieve even before she entered the Greenwood Institute in Lusaka, Zambia, to begin her journalism training. She calls it "solution-seeking journalism," and she has never wavered from it. It is an approach to journalism that may not win her admirers among those in power—which tells her she must be doing something right. The process begins with her identifying a problem from an array of psychosocial ills invariably affecting less privileged people in Zambian society. Next, she uses her platform as a television presenter to broadcast this problem to the population at large. Many journalists would stop here, but she does not. What comes after is the advocacy component, pursuing positive change with badger-like intensity.

To understand where this resolve comes from, let us go back to Kumwenda's childhood. She grew up in a country bedeviled by gender-based violence. Rape, defilement (which Kumwenda explained is the sexual molestation of children under

Above: *For 15 years, television reporter and aspiring lawyer Mwape Kumwenda has been practicing what she calls "solution seeking journalism" on behalf of the less privileged people of Zambia.*

fifteen years of age), and life-threatening battery were common and mostly went unpunished. At the time, the courts did not pursue cases because the overwhelming majority of women and girls—the children were mostly girls—could not afford legal representation. Moreover, many of the abused women were related to, and often dependent on, the perpetrators, which made them reluctant to report the assault. Not only was justice being denied to many thousands of victims each year, but the enduring effects of sexual violence hindered women advancing their careers. The extent of this crisis was captured in a damning 2012 report sponsored by Cornell University titled "They are Destroying Our Futures: Sexual Violence Against Girls in Zambia's Schools."

This threat was the backdrop to Kumwenda's school years. She recalls singing in her school choir, which brought her into contact with drama groups and choirs from other schools. They were asked to compose and perform songs to do with gender-based violence. And as part of this process of educating the youth of Zambia about the dangers they faced, victims of sexual assault were invited to share their stories and experiences. "I was deeply touched by this," she remembers.

Kumwenda's mother was also determined to make her daughter aware of the risks she faced as a schoolgirl. Kumwenda had an older brother and three younger brothers. In time, two sisters would be born, but the age differences were such that Kumwenda essentially grew up surrounded by boys. Being the only girl meant she was the focus of much of her mother's understandable anxiety: "My mother was very strict about how I related to men," she told me.

When Kumwenda began her work as a journalist fifteen years back, she confronted head-on the twin challenges of rampant sexual violence in Zambian society and the virtual impunity that perpetrators enjoyed. Her television reportage was integral to Zambian media becoming

Kumwenda at a stool-making section outside Chifundo market, Lusaka, Zambia.

Most media organizations in Zambia are partly owned by business people who have connections to ministers or financial dealings with the party in power. To maintain complete independence, Kumwenda and a colleague started their own company, Crown TV.

an agent for change by giving a voice and a face to victims, bringing a taboo topic out the shadows, exposing perpetrators to the harsh light of public opinion, and thereby spurring government authorities into taking action. As a result of her advocacy, police are now stationed in hospitals to deal expeditiously with sexual-assault cases. The government has established fast-track courts to ensure perpetrators do not escape justice by endless postponement and delays to court procedures—a favorite tactic used in the past to circumvent accountability. Victim support units have been set up. And importantly, traditional leaders in rural regions, whose tribal sway can exceed the influence of the central government, have been brought into the fold to support these initiatives.

Many abused women and girls have been helped by Kumwenda. She cites the case of a fourteen-year-old girl victimized by a prophet. Self-styled prophets claim to receive messages directly from God and as such are respected members of Zambian society, often allied to churches. Their special powers are supposed to include, among others, divining the future, discerning a person's hidden thoughts, and making spiritual diagnoses to explain negative life events, such as illness or the breakup of a marriage. This formidable array of self-professed capabilities gives them a profound hold over their believers and considerable influence within their communities.

None of this deterred Kumwenda. Her reporting revealed that the girl in question had been raped, acquired a sexually transmitted disease, and fallen pregnant. Her exposé of the child's trauma and the perpetrator played a pivotal role in the prophet receiving a fifteen-year jail sentence. When the prophet took his appeal to the Supreme Court, Kumwenda tracked the case, keeping it in the court of public opinion and using her coverage of the trial to negate the power differential between child and rapist. The sentence was upheld.

If the exhortations of her mother sensitized Kumwenda to one societal ill, the work of her father highlighted another: endemic corruption. As an auditor employed by the government, he repeatedly unearthed evidence of government sleaze and financial irregularities, which he meticulously outlined in his reports. But there was seldom any accountability. Kumwenda saw how devastated her father was by the government's failure to act and address corruption. She has never forgotten his mounting frustration at his impotence in bringing about change. To her, journalism could be the vessel that provided the missing piece of accountability.

Corruption spawns numerous social and economic ills and blights local communities in Zambia. Two examples given by Kumwenda are the absence of clean water to drink and poor-quality education. To tackle this, she has set about exposing the misuse of public funds. One high-profile case entailed whistleblowers alerting Kumwenda to the fact that a large amount of money earmarked by the government for community projects had been misappropri-ated. She was given a trove of documents to prove the allegations, and she set about verifying the evidence while guaranteeing anonymity for the informers. Her report was instrumental in the arrests of member of Parliament Rodgers Mwewa and his wife, Anne Mwitwa, a government official.

Kumwenda's prominent public profile as a television reporter coupled with her advocacy for the less privileged in society has garnered her a wide viewership. She told me the story of a mother taking her desperately sick child from the hospital directly to the television studio and asking for help. The child required a surgical procedure that could not be undertaken in Zambia. A hospital in India had offered its services, but bureaucratic incompetence and callous indifference had for years combined to stall the mother's passport application. Now, her child was dying, and she saw Mwape Kumwenda as her last hope. Moved by the woman's plight, Kumwenda petitioned the minister of community development. She lobbied for funding.

The child got to India. A few years later, she received a surprise phone call from a grateful mother; her daughter, now restored to health, had just started school.

Giving a voice to the underdog can, on occasion, prove harrowing. Kumwenda was a lone voice reporting on a long-running land dispute that pitted the government against a local community deemed to be squatting on land earmarked for military officers. More than two thousand people had lived there for fifty years—their ancestors were buried on the land. When soldiers opened fire on unarmed protesters upset at their imminent eviction, Kumwenda suddenly found herself a first responder and witness to the aftermath of a shooting that left one man dead and another dying in front of her.

The violence did not end there. Doing a follow-up story the next day, she visited the funeral home where the leader of the opposition was also paying a visit. They were physically set upon there by a mob of government supporters. Mourners were beaten, a colleague had his camera stolen, and Kumwenda had to lock herself and her cameraman in a room in the funeral home to escape the attack. Undeterred, she still did not let up in her coverage of the dispute. The minister of defence at the time called her out, asking why she persisted in questioning the authorities. Her answer went to the heart of her journalism: accountability. Two innocent people had been killed, children had been left fatherless and an unemployed mother was suddenly widowed and destitute, forced to give up two of her four young children to the care of others.

Kumwenda kept asking how such a situation had come to pass. Other journalists were cowed when it came to challenging the government and army. In the end, the authorities conceded, and a substantial portion of the land was returned to the community. "To some extent, I feel that my persistent reporting helped shelter the local people," she told me.

The violence she witnessed, however, left her emotionally traumatized. Gory images of blood and brains spilling out onto the ground and the wailing of relatives and children at the scene of the killings stayed with her in the weeks that followed. Realizing she needed help and finding solace in religion, she turned to her pastor rather than a psychologist for therapy.

The language that Kumwenda uses to describe her reporting is informative when dissected within the framework of moral injury: "As the Fourth Estate, we have a duty to provide checks and balances to those in authority to do the right thing," she explained. "If we remain silent when faced by these issues, then social and economic injustices remain the order of the day. And then we too are guilty of not providing a proper service to the people. We owe it to them."

In this powerful declaration of intent, we can see that doing nothing in the face of morally egregious behavior is not an option, for an act of omission becomes tainted by guilt. When Kumwenda links guilt with inaction, she brings into focus a key behavior and a primary emotion associated with moral injury. But for her, this is only the first half of the equation. The part that comes next, the part that eluded her father, is the power to bring about change.

"Unless the evil of people is exposed, they will continue with it," she goes on. "But when they are exposed, they are shamed by their wrongdoing. And then there is room for change." In these ringing words, we are introduced to another key behavior and emotion associated with moral injury. We have the act of committing something morally egregious, be it corruption or rape. And when this is exposed, shame follows in the wake. Shame is the impetus for change—the antidote to inaction. That the change is enforced and not necessarily accompanied by repentance on the part of the perpetrators does not dilute the outcome. More often than not, it is the "system" that is being prodded and shamed into providing justice for those who lack the clout to obtain it, like the sexually abused schoolgirl left with gonorrhea and a baby to nurse, or the downtrodden community forced to drink filthy water.

When parsing what Kumwenda has to say to explain her motivation, I should note that she makes no direct mention of moral injury. Like many journalists, this is not a concept that she is familiar with. But her choice of words is telling, for it unconsciously reflects the key principles that define the condition.

What is equally telling in this context are the principles to which she adheres in her reporting. She sees her journalism as "centered on the truth." She was at pains in explaining to me that she is careful not to pass judgement in her stories. Rather, she lets the facts alone convey the message. That they can prove so damning speaks to the power of unadorned truth. She is proud that précis of her reports are used as evidence by law-enforcement officials.

Zambia ranks 109 out of 180 countries on the Reporters Without Borders press freedom index. Journalists are not murdered, doxed, or routinely incarcerated, but the country's lowly position on the list is indicative of the challenges they face operating freely. The problem, according to Kumwenda, is often one of conflict of interests. Most media organizations are partly owned by businesspeople who have connections to ministers or financial dealings with the party in power. They are fearful of losing their broadcasting license and revenue if they report unfavorably on the government. As a result, they self-censor.

In 2019, after spending thirteen years at Muvi-TV, Kumwenda left when the owner went into politics. She was worried the station would not be seen as credible. Her move to Prime TV ended two years later when the government revoked their license, complaining that the station's reports were too opinionated. The license was only returned after a change in government. So to maintain complete independence, she and a colleague started their own company, Crown TV.

"I make sure the company's paperwork and taxes are pristine," she told me, citing the case of a private newspaper silenced by bogus tax claims. She is constantly wary of government intimidation, noting that her industry is regulated by the Independent

Broadcasting Authority, whose board is appointed by the government and answers to them. Independence in this case is therefore a misnomer, and while legislation has been drafted to address this issue, she noted ruefully that politicians control this process, too.

All of which brings us back to where we started. Fifteen years into her career as a journalist, Kumwenda is again planning on pursuing her first career choice: law. Her motivation is not disillusionment with journalism—just the opposite. She wants to be in a position in which she can provide her own legal counsel to her fledgling television company. The specter of conflict of interests looms once more, but this time pertaining to lawyers who may have undisclosed political links or government-dependent business interests that could bias their opinions.

Driven by a fierce moral courage to pursue her advocacy work, she sees a natural synergy between journalism and the law. But first, both have to escape the officious tentacles of those in power.

Naing in the living room of his home in exile. Oslo, Norway.

Aye Chan Naing

When Myanmarese journalist Aye Chan Naing was twenty-two years of age, he did something remarkable. Two months shy of completing dental school and with the prospect of a financially comfortable life ahead of him, he slipped quietly away from his family home in Yangon. Accompanied by three friends, he crossed the border into Thailand hoping to join an insurgency against his government.

There were no family farewells. Instead, Naing left a note for his parents explaining his reasons for leaving and saying he would be back in six months. Driven by a fierce moral courage given wings by the impetuosity of youth, he could not have known that twenty-four years would pass before he saw Burma, soon to be renamed Myanmar, again.

He left behind a country roiled by political unrest. The 8888 uprising—started by students on August 8, 1988—had spread nationwide to involve hundreds of thousands of citizens from all walks of life. They were protesting against the totalitarian government of General Ne Win and his Burma Socialist Programme Party, whose Soviet-style economic policies had impoverished the country.

There were myriad other grievances, too. To Naing and fellow dissidents, the protests were also about the stranglehold on society exerted by a brutal military, the necessity of having military connections if one wanted to get on in life, and the corruption, nepotism, and lack of justice that such a system spawned. A bloody military coup on September 18 put an end to the

Above: When the independent broadcast media group, the Democratic Voice of Burma (DVB), passed one million subscribers on YouTube, Naing received this golden plaque recognizing his achievement.

unrest. Thousands of citizens were killed.

The Naing family was at the epicenter of this discontent, which had simmered for years. The family's home was within the grounds of RASU, the Rangoon Arts and Sciences University, a hotbed of dissent. Naing's parents held faculty appointments there. In the home, education was prized, and political talk, invariably critical of the government, a surreptitious dinner-table discussion. It was simply too dangerous to speak openly in a country ruled with an iron fist.

Young Aye Chan's memories of childhood contain moments of high political drama. He was nine years of age when U Thant, the Burmese Secretary General of the United Nations, died in New York City on November 25, 1974. When U Thant was denied a state funeral, incensed students from RASU snatched his repatriated body from the funeral procession and brought it onto the university campus to hold their own ceremony for him. A literal tug-of-war over the corpse ensued between rival student factions and the government before

the army stormed the university grounds to end the standoff.

The boy witnessed these dramatic events from his apartment. He saw demonstrators killed. He remembers his parents making food for the student protestors. He recalls tanks rolling down the road beneath his widow at 3 a.m., searchlights probing his apartment, the military barking out commands to shut the curtains or be shot. Such memories fused with dinner-table talk to awaken Naing's political consciousness. With all avenues to peaceful dissent blocked, he came to see armed insurrection as the only way to bring about change.

No sooner had he crossed the Thailand border than he met with exiled leaders from Burma's ethnic groups—the Mon, Kachin, and Chin, among others. To his dismay, he found them "living in a bubble," surprisingly uninformed of the 8888 uprising. The absence of foreign news organizations in Burma coupled with the government's total control of the media had effectively insulated the country. Naing could not have known it then, but in time, as he found his career path, his efforts would become instrumental in bringing news of Burma not only to the wider world, but to the Burmese themselves.

Prior to leaving Yangon, Naing had been given the name and telephone number of a single contact: Swedish journalist and author Bertil Lintner, Burma correspondent of the now-defunct *Far Eastern Economic Review* and an expert on Burmese affairs. It is no exaggeration to say the call Naing made changed the course of his life. "Bertil's wife—Hseng Noung—answered the phone," he recalls. "She invited me to visit them in Bangkok. So I did. I lived with them for the next three years."

Lintner was keen to interview exiled Burmese. Naing was his conduit to them, setting up meetings and interpreting and translating what they had to say. In the process of watching and learning from Lintner, he became a journalist. He began learning English, studying at the British Council, and boosting his skills by reading English newspapers. He joined the All Burma Students' Democratic Front (ABSDF) and started a bimonthly publication, the *DAWN News Bulletin*, together with Max Ediger, an American running an NGO. Their focus was on human rights violations.

All the while, he was living without documentation in Bangkok. When Lintner's landlord threatened to alert the authorities to this fact, the Lintner family promptly found another place to live and took their unregistered guest with them. Naing calls his mentor "a remarkable man."

In 1991, Naing attended a weeklong Human Rights Conference in Germany. During his return trip, he stepped unwittingly into the pages of a John le Carré thriller. Airline officials from Sabena, Naing's carrier, became suspicious of his travel documents. Sections of his passport were highlighted and the document stamped as fraudulent. He was nevertheless allowed to board the plane for the trip to Bangkok.

Terrified of being detained on arrival and sent back to Myanmar, where he faced torture and likely execution, Naing tried to erase the highlights with whiskey. His hand was shaking so much that airline attendants took pity on him. Learning of his grave predicament, they told him to drink the whiskey instead while they set about removing the highlights and stamp with liquor and razor blades.

On arrival in Bangkok airport, he heard his name called over the public-address system. He saw the police mistakenly detain another traveler, believing it to be him. Not trusting his doctored passport, Naing bribed some airport cleaners to given him their clothes so he could escape. But he ended up instead in the departure lounge where he remained for three days, making desperate phone calls to friends and colleagues. The crisis only resolved when the German ambassador to Thailand arrived with a plane ticket to Germany. Given this opening to freedom, Naing applied for asylum.

His stay in Germany was brief. The ABSDF wanted to open an office in Europe. Sweden agreed to host it, so Naing moved there to help set up operations. In 1992, he relocated to Norway, assigned by the Myanmarese government in exile—the National Coalition Government of the Union of Burma—to set up DVB, the Democratic Voice of Burma. This nonprofit radio station was funded by agencies in Norway, Sweden, and the United States. Getting a shortwave radio station in Norway was critical to DVB's success. Prior to that, opposition groups had run smaller mobile radio stations out of the jungle on the Myanmar–Thailand border where they were vulnerable to attack. Establishing DVB operations in Norway essentially placed the station beyond the reach of the country's junta.

Naing viewed DVB's mandate as providing "real information on Burma. . . . No one knew what the truth was," he explained, "because the government controlled the news, the narrative of what was happening with the opposition. We in Burma don't just live by our nose for breathing. We live by our ears. Hearing your radio station was very strong."

Over the next decade, Naing worked assiduously to establish DVB and expand its reach. To counteract the station's growing influence, the Myanmarese government resorted to subterfuge, dispatching

The journalist flips through his history in this photo album while in exile at his home. Oslo, Norway.

In April 2022, Naing revisited Oslo City Hall where he had attended the Nobel Peace Prize ceremony for Aung San Suu Kyi in 1991.

spies to Norway to lure him back home. He never took the bait.

Things in Myanmar began looking up in 2010. A general election presaged democratic reforms. The military junta was dissolved one year later, succeeded by a nominally civilian government albeit one still under the eagle eye of the generals. By 2012, a thaw in government repression allowed DVB's network of underground journalists to come above ground and start reporting openly. Naing led this transition. The radio station's offices in Norway were shut. Married and with children by now, he moved operations and his family to Thailand. Five years later, he felt optimistic enough to relocate work and home to Myanmar. It would prove a false dawn.

Myanmar's fragile democratic progress unraveled when the result of the 2020 election was declared invalid by the Tatmadaw, the country's armed forces. Naing and his family were back in Norway when the military launched a coup a few months later. This was followed by the brutal suppression of dissent. The United Nations Human Rights Office estimates that at least 1,500 people have been killed since the coup, including 200 tortured to death in military custody. Over 10,000 people have been detained.

A nascent, free press was an early casualty of the crackdown. The military blocked TV stations, disrupted the internet, banned news organizations, and arrested many journalists, including seven from DVB. The DVB TV station was officially banned on March 8, 2021. In response, Naing has been in the process of taking DVB global—broadcasting online from offices and virtual hubs in Australia, the United States, and Canada—and using a citizen-journalist network across Myanmar, providing daily accounts of the army's lethal suppression of protestors.

"We still want to fight back," Naing told me, "but things in Burma have never been harder than now. The military cannot go beyond the current darkness." Three decades of resistance have left Naing unbowed and defiant. But he is older now and looking to the next generation of journalist-activists to take up the mantle. He sees one of his chief tasks as "getting the youngsters out the country." And with an eye on history and his own personal experience, he exhorts them to play the long game. "I thought I would be back after six months," he reminds them, "and it took over twenty years."

Naing's journey from budding dentist in Yangon to chief executive officer of a banned radio station 8,000 kilometers away in Oslo, the far-flung beacon of democracy and freedom to his troubled land, is testimony to his resilience and conviction. His accomplishments have garnered accolades, such as a prestigious International Press Freedom Award in 2021 from the Committee to Protect Journalists.

And yet, impressive as these achievement are, external markers of a lifetime's tortuous journey tell only part of the story. What escapes the glare of public recognition is another journey, arguably more extraordinary—for without it, none of these successes are possible. Naing undertook it out of sight, in solitude, alone with his thoughts and fears, often in the small hours of the morning. It entailed a personal struggle that was painful, testing the limits of familial bonds, parental love, filial respect, and proving the ultimate test of his moral courage.

When Naing's parents found the note that he had left informing them of his flight, they immediately set out in pursuit, determined to head him off and bring him home. Through mutual contacts, they latched on to his movements. But the trail ran cold and their son slipped through their despairing fingers. Naing's love for his mother was such that he resisted contacting her for the next five years. He knew that if she asked him to return, he would not be able to say no.

Let us pause for a moment and reflect on this. Put yourself in this young man's shoes and try and fathom the depth of this resolve. And as you do so, marvel at his mother's response to her son's actions when they next spoke after all those years of silence. "Don't come back!" were her first words. "You have done something you believe in. Finish it. If you come back in the middle, you will be welcome from our back

"My struggle is nothing," maintains Naing. "Millions have given more."

door, not our front one." There was awe in Naing's voice when he relayed these words to me. "Can you imagine that?" he asked me. "I am so proud of my mother!" And then he lapsed into silence, overcome by the memory of it all.

When Naing set out for the Thailand border as a young man, his life irrevocably changed. With the cockiness of youth, he thought he was in control of his destiny, but the grand play of political events determined otherwise. What sustained him when his plans went awry was his moral courage. Inaction—a failure to respond to the injustices of life under the boot of a junta—was not an option. He has held to his moral compass ever since. That his path was made easier by his parents coming in time to follow the same lodestar cannot paper over the pain they all must have felt at a wrenching separation.

"My struggle is nothing," Naing said as I took him step by step over the course of his life. "Millions have given more. I have paid a price, but I have been recognized. Others have sacrificed a lot more without recogni-

tion." When he feels depressed by events, he admonishes himself: "I should not be complaining at all. Think of your country, not yourself. Our listeners needs us."

He also has no regrets about turning his back on six years of study and a career in dentistry. He laughingly notes that when he left his country, he was also leaving behind the prospect of a Porsche or Tesla in the garage. But then he turned serious again: "Living in an oppressive situation and being educated and rich—there is no luxury in that."

Aye Chan Naing's riches now are more abstract. They include the pride his parents and siblings have taken in his accomplishments and the thanks of fellow Myanmarese people for keeping them informed of what is going on in their oppressed country. "You changed our nation," they have told him, and there is no hyperbole in this.

As our interview came to a close, he briefly excused himself and returned to show me a gold plaque. It was given to him by YouTube, in recognition of DVB reaching a million subscribers.

Figueredo Ruíz in his home in exile. West Philadelphia, PA, USA.

Cándido Figueredo Ruíz

For twenty-four years and eight months, Cándido Figueredo Ruíz was marked for death. To thwart the bullets of his eager assassins, the Paraguayan journalist lived surrounded by seven heavily armed guards. Two patrolled the front of his modest home, two took up station in the short corridor outside his bedroom, and three kept an eye on his back door. Simple pleasures such as sitting on the veranda on a warm evening, going for a stroll down the street, attending a birthday party or wedding, enjoying a cup of coffee at a local café, or dining in a restaurant were considered too risky. When he traveled by car, two bodyguards went with him, while the others followed in a second vehicle close behind.

Figueredo Ruíz lived this extraordinary existence because he was a journalist who dared to tell inconvenient truths. It really all came down to drugs and geography.

He was born in Pedro Juan Caballero, Paraguay, a city of 230,000 people that straddles the border with Brazil. Nearby is the largest marijuana plantation in South America. The city also lies along the lucrative corridor used to transport cocaine through Colombia and Bolivia to markets in the United States. Poorly monitored by law enforcement agencies over the years, the area historically has been a haven for smugglers of illegal cigarettes, guns, and electronics.

In the wake of drugs came corruption —a hydra of graft, extortion, bribery, double-dealing, and profiteering. It snaked its way up from the petty criminals and lowly dealers through the customs officials, police, and lawyers into the corridors of power where politicians on the take

Above: Figueredo Ruíz and his wife Luz Patricia Bellenzier, stand on the deck of their home in exile in West Philadelphia.

dispensed their largesse or displeasure according to self-interest. The people were poor. Drug money was plentiful. Brutality and poverty locked the system in place. To a journalist with a strong moral compass and steely resolve like Figueredo Ruíz, there was no shortage of truths to tell.

He came to journalism relatively late in life. One of six children in a modest, working-class family, he grew up in a country ruled with an iron fist by Alfonso Stroessner, a dictator of mixed German and Paraguayan descent with a fondness for Nazi fugitives and a taste for great cruelty.

As a child, Figueredo Ruíz was an avid reader and drawn to the arts. He had hoped to go to university and pursue a career in journalism, but gaining entry entailed taking a pledge of loyalty to Stroessner. He balked at this—a decision that showed early signs of the independence and determination that would come to define his later career.

At eighteen, with his pathway to university blocked, Figueredo Ruíz fell in love with a Norwegian girl visiting Paraguay,

married her, and went to live in Norway. In doing so, he wryly notes, he moved from one of the world's most repressive countries to one of the freest.

At first, Norway seemed like paradise to him, a "comfortable country [that] took care of its citizens from birth to death." Soon there was a family to support, and he found work monitoring machinery in an iron-processing factory. It was a far cry from journalism, and the schedule, which included night shifts, was tough, but the money was good and the work secure.

He remained in Norway for twenty-one years. By the time Figueredo Ruíz's marriage failed, Stroessner had been deposed in a coup, gone into exile in Brazil, and the press in Paraguay was being unshackled. Much as he admired Norwegian society, Figueredo Ruíz had never felt fully at ease in it. It was time to return home.

As an added sweetener to his homecoming, Figueredo Ruíz landed his first journalism position, directing Radio Yby Yau, a small radio station in Concepción, 200 kilometers from his hometown. Two

Figueredo Ruíz in his home office, with his armed guards, who were a constant presence given the risk of assassination. Pedro Juan Caballero, Paraguay.

months later, he was back in Pedro Juan Caballero working for *ABC Color*, one of Paraguay's most widely read daily newspapers. It was fitting that a man who had refused to bend a knee to Stroessner was now working for a newspaper the dictator had once shuttered for dissent.

It did not take long for Figueredo Ruíz to file his first corruption story. He learned about contraband beer coming into the country and the payoffs the police were receiving from customs officials. He found the bodega where the beer was stored and photographed it. Just before he was about to break the story, he was approached by a high-profile lawyer with judicial connections representing the company flouting the law and offered two thousand dollars to back off.

Determined to expose the multiple layers of graft involved, Figueredo Ruíz set up another meeting with the lawyer, filming what went down with a miniature camcorder hidden in his clothes. On camera, he asked for the payoff to increase to three thousand dollars, considered a small fortune in Paraguay at the time. The cash was immediately produced. "What would you like me to say in my article?" he asked obsequiously, handing the lawyer a piece of blank paper and pen. The lawyer obliged, and Figueredo had him read the note aloud. The whole interaction was caught on camera, filmed amid the piles of incriminating cash. The following day, Figueredo Ruíz's scoop was on the front page of *ABC Color*. He also let it be known that he had given the three thousand dollars to a children's ward at a local hospital.

Three days later, the front of his house was sprayed with forty-five bullets. If that message was not clear enough, anonymous callers also told him his days were numbered. *ABC Color* responded by publishing news of how their man in Pedro Juan Caballero was being threatened. The intimidation of Cándido Figueredo Ruíz now became the main news item of the day. His cause was taken up the Committee to Protect Journalists in New York.

With international attention on the country, Paraguayan authorities responded by assigning guards to keep a constant watch over the journalist, twenty-four hours a day, seven days a week. Sixteen cameras were installed within and around his home. Such were the gravity of the threats, Figueredo Ruíz was trained to use firearms—an unthinkable option for journalists—lest his security detail be overwhelmed. Overnight, his life changed irrevocably. He did not know it then, but he would never again walk freely in the city of his birth.

Figueredo Ruíz's response to the intimidation was to double down and keep exposing corruption. "I grew up seeing injustice," he told me. More than two decades after refusing to swear fealty to the Stroessner regime, an act that cost him a university education, Figueredo Ruíz's moral compass remained unwavering. "I have always been a rebel," he declared. "I will not kneel to power."

There is nothing new in journalists being threatened with death. What makes Figueredo Ruíz's experience so unusual is the degree to which these threats, and the measures taken to thwart them, have over-turned his life. There were only two rooms in his house that were off limit to the guards: his bedroom and the washroom. "It was awful—terrible at first," he recalled. Having remarried, his worries extended to his wife, 500 kilometers away in the capital, Asunción, where she was studying psychology while working part time for *ABC Color.* "We know where she is," anonymous callers insinuated ominously. "She is so beautiful . . ." Three policewomen were assigned to guard her, too.

While his wife was spared, Figueredo Ruíz's immediate family was not. "Let me tell you a story that is very sad to me," he offered when I asked about them. He recounted how a local bank robbery ended with one of the robbers and a teller dying. Figueredo Ruíz learned that the mastermind behind the botched attempt had been one Luis Enrique Georges, a killer so notorious that people feared mentioning his name. Figueredo Ruíz, on the other hand, had no such qualms, outing the man in his account of the robbery. Georges's response was to kidnap Figueredo Ruíz's

Figueredo Ruiz goes for 15-kilometer walks every day, unaccompanied, exulting in his newfound freedom.

brother and threaten to execute him and thereafter kill Figueredo Ruíz's four sisters, his mother, and all their cats and dogs, if he did not divulge his sources. Figueredo Ruíz's counter-response, made under the intense pressure of a thirty-minute deadline, was to phone Georges and thank him. "To this day, I don't know where this came from," he said. "But I told him I would be very thankful and asked him when he was going to begin. 'To me, it means absolutely nothing, because my family only create problems,'" he recalled saying. "You are doing me a favor. Do it!"

Listening to Figueredo Ruíz's account of this remarkable interaction, I thought of the psychotherapeutic technique of paradoxical intention, pioneered by the celebrated psychiatrist Viktor Frankl. Here, the therapeutic aim is to circumvent the consequences of anticipatory anxiety by encouraging the individual to *increase* the anxiety-provoking thought or action previously avoided. It is, however, one thing to apply this construct in therapy, but quite another to stop a known killer from mur-

dering your relative. Figueredo Ruíz, of course, never had Viktor Frankl in mind when he instinctively blurted out his outrageous challenge, but he is convinced it worked. His brother was freed, at the cost of the journalist promising to write a flattering article on Georges' life.

The kidnapping marked another turning point in Figueredo Ruíz's life. All contact with his siblings was then severed. He never saw them again. They were instructed to disown him if ever asked about him. His remaining contact with his elderly mother was reduced to fleeting moments in the driveway to her home, mother and son surrounded by a phalanx of armed men.

Figueredo Ruíz is an ebullient man who appears younger than his sixty-six years. He has a disarming, upbeat manner with a quick sense of humor. This jolly persona, while true to his character, also obscures the many dark and desperate times he endured. Only once did his facade crumble during our interview, when I asked him to reflect on the personal price paid. He sat silently, his facial expression somber at first before the weight of what he had been through year upon year slowly unraveled his composure and tears eased speech aside.

"There were days when I did not want to leave my room," he recalled, drying his eyes, "because the first thing I would see was a cop saying, 'Good morning, sir—everything calm here.' And then there would be another cop in my study. I would ask my wife to bring my coffee into the bedroom. I could not face the reality of our existence. But we had to pull ourselves up. Nobody else could." All the while, he kept reminding himself and his wife that they were doing important work, even as they came to the end of each month with almost no money. "We could make the rich and powerful tremble. We were the stone in their shoe that made them uncomfortable. I had to hold on to this because if I sat down and thought about my situation, it would bring me down."

Over the years, the attacks never let up. His home was raked with gunfire on two further occasions. His car was shot up twice. During his decades of confinement, six Paraguayan journalists were killed, including Pablo Medina Velázquez, his colleague at *ABC Color*. Figueredo Ruíz recalls being sent a photograph of the murdered journalist crumpled in his car, head down, blood dripping. And then there were times when those arrested because of what Figueredo Ruíz had written would be released within days and drive past his house honking their horns.

When I asked Figueredo Ruíz if he thought about death, he said plainly: "I have lived next to death every day." The murder rate in Pedro Juan Caballero is high, and he has seen a lot of dead people; tortured, dismembered, burned—so many different ways of being killed. "I have a photographic archive that cannot be published because it is too gruesome," he revealed. "My greatest fear was that I would be captured, tortured, and cut into pieces."

On February 12, 2020, gunmen walked into the home of journalist Lourenco Veras in Pedro Juan Caballero and shot him

Figueredo Ruíz, who carried a weapon for protection, with two of his armed guards.

eleven times, killing him while he was having dinner with his family. The killers let it be known Figueredo Ruíz was next on their list. Emotionally spent, the intrepid journalist had had enough. A year shy of retirement, and with an offer to join a friend in Pennsylvania, he and his wife packed up and left Paraguay. He arrived in the United States just as COVID-19 stay-at-home orders were announced. After twenty-four years in lockdown, he laughingly told his host he felt right at home.

Figueredo Ruízcarries the scars of his prolonged ordeal. When he hears the occasional gunshot in the Pennsylvanian night, he reflexively reaches for a weapon no longer there. His responses are automatic, conditioned by years in the crosshairs of the *sicarios*. With the easing of pandemic restrictions, he goes for 15-kilometer walks every day, unaccompanied, exulting in his newfound freedom. These long walks, however, are also an attempt to shed the hypervigilance that stalks his waking hours, the need to constantly look over his shoulder and check whether he is safe.

This physiological marker of emotional trauma, hardwired into his autonomic nervous system and geared for survival, is difficult to extinguish. But these phenomena, learned involuntarily, are offset by a happier offshoot of his experiences under siege. The man who was denied the education he wanted because he would not betray his moral compass is now an honored guest in the lecture halls of great American universities such as Columbia and Princeton. Figueredo Ruíz smiled as he told me this—and in his expression, there was a touch of wonder, too.

Above: *Politkovskaya. Moscow, Russia.*

Anna Politkovskaya

For the final profile in this book, I return to Russia, a vast country spanning eleven time zones, controlled by one man, Vladimir Putin. I do so because as I write, this country, with the world's largest nuclear arsenal and a dictatorial leader, is waging war on neighboring Ukraine, illegally annexing territory, laying waste to towns and cities, torturing, killing, and abducting civilians. The Russian journalist who I am about to profile was born to Ukrainian parents. She would have opposed this war and President Putin with every fiber of her being.

In doing so, she would have known that Russians who challenge their president today do so at their peril. Dissent from high-profile opponents has been met with a bullet in the head, a lethal nerve agent like Novichok, or lengthy incarceration in a remote prison that harkens back to the Gulag. The brazenness of these responses perpetrated a stone's throw from the Kremlin in the case of politician Boris Nemtsov, or onboard a jetliner as with opposition leader Alexei Navalny, or on the quiet streets of Salisbury, England, as with double agent Sergei Skripal and his daughter Yulia, acts as its own kind of warning. Nobody and nowhere are safe. It, therefore, takes a person of rare courage to write this:

> "Why do I have it in for Putin? . . . Because of his crudeness which is worse than thieving. Because of his cynicism. Because of his racism. Because of endless war. Because of

Above: *Politkovskaya at work in her office.*

[225]

lies. Because of the gas at Nord-Ost.* Because of corpses of the innocently killed, accompanying his entire first term as president. Corpses that might have been avoided."

The woman who wrote these incandescent words was the journalist Anna Politkovskaya. She had a lot more to say about President Putin, whom she assailed relentlessly until she was silenced in a contract killing. The date of her assassination was October 7, 2006. President Putin's birthday happens to fall on October 7, too.

Much has been written about Anna Politkovskaya. In the West, she was celebrated while she was alive and lionized after her death. Within Russia, the government's rigid control of the media meant she was, and likely still is, relatively unknown to the majority of her fellow citizens. To those in the Russian media, her star shines as brightly as it does abroad, but the public peans of praise are muted or absent there for obvious reasons. Russian history reveals that assassination can spread like a contagion. Politkovskaya was only too aware of this. She foretold her own death at the funeral of her poisoned colleague, Yuri Shchekochikhin, in July 2003. That certainty, however, never stopped her reportage. Readers everywhere marveled at her courage even as they wondered as to the source of it.

Anna Politkovskaya was born Anna Stepanovna Mazepa to Ukrainian parents. The name Mazepa is steeped in Ukrainian history. Ivan Mazepa (1639–1709) served as hetman or head of state of a Cossack region and militarily opposed Tsar Peter the Great. Like many Ukrainians, her family suffered under Stalin's ruinous policy of forced collectivization of the country's farms, but with the succession of Nikita

---

* The reference to the gas at Nord-Ost is a damning critique of a hostage rescue attempt on October 26, 2002, when Russian special forces pumped a fentanyl derivative into the ventilation system of a Moscow theatre in which 40 Chechen extremists were holding 850 hostages. In the ensuing firefight, all the insurgents were killed. While the exact death toll among the hostages remains uncertain, it is estimated that the toxic gas killed at least 130 of them.

Khrushchev as first secretary of the Communist Party of the Soviet Union, their fortunes changed. Khrushchev grew up in the Ukraine, had a Ukrainian wife, and retained his affection for the country and its culture. Politkovskaya's father, Stepan, who was a foreign policy analyst and her mother, Raisa, an academic, were appointed to serve with the Ukrainian delegation at the United Nations in New York City, which is where their daughter Anna was born. When the family was recalled to Moscow in 1964, they were by then part of the nomenklatura, those members of the Communist party who enjoyed special material privileges.

I never had the opportunity to interview Politkovskaya, unfortunately, but from my reading of numerous articles describing her career, there were no clues early on that hinted at the formidable journalist she would later become. She graduated from Moscow State University's School of Journalism in 1980, five years before Mikhail Gorbachev's policies of perestroika (reconstruction) and glasnost (transparency) began transforming the Soviet Union. By then, she was married to fellow journalist Alexander "Sasha" Politkovsky and the mother of two young children. For the next decade, she pursued an undistinguished career writing for *Isvestia*, *Air Transport*—the magazine of Russia's national air carrier, Aeroflot—and *Megapolis-Express*, while the career of her husband soared as presenter of the popular late-night TV program, *Vzglyad*.

Things picked up professionally for her in 1994 when she joined the cultural affairs section of *Obshchaya Gazeta*, a liberal weekly newspaper established three years earlier during a momentous period that saw the toppling of President Gorbachev, the dissolution of the USSR, and the election of President Yeltsin. She began profiling the lives of artists and the Russian intelligentsia, gaining ready access to their world as the well-off daughter of diplomats and wife of a celebrated TV personality. The year 1994 was also the start of the First Chechen War. That two years of warfare largely passed her by is indica-

Politkovskaya presents her book, In Putin's Russia, *at the Leipzig Book Fair. Leipzig, Germany.*

tive of how far and quickly her focus would later shift, from the rarefied world of privilege in a crumbling Soviet Union to the worst of privations in the charnel house of Chechnya when the Second Chechen War began in 1999.

The reasons behind Politkovskaya's radical, rapid transformation from cultural to conflict reporter are the source of enduring mystery and debate. And wonder, too, given the unflinching, self-sacrificing degree to which she exposed human rights abuses perpetrated by Russian forces during the war.

Terry Gould, in his book *Marked for Death*,* tells the story of six journalists murdered for doing their job and devotes one of the chapters to Politkovskaya. In his search to understand what drove her to expose the horrors of the Second Chechen War, he relates an episode that occurred on August 27, 1996. On that Tuesday morning, Politkovskaya visited the office of Civil Assistance, a refugee center in Mos-

cow. She was hoping to write a cover story on Chechen children entering a Moscow elementary school for the first time. She never found the children she was looking before, but instead came face to face with scores of desperate, wounded, and traumatized Chechen refugees shoe-horned into the corridors, who had lost parents, children, husbands, and wives in the conflict and who had traveled for days without food and proper sanitation to get to the center for assistance.

To Svetlana Gannushkina, the director of Civil Assistance, this was Politkovskaya's epiphany. Moved by what she saw, the elegant, fashionable, well-dressed Politkovskaya rolled up her sleeves and began helping the center's staff draw up a list of the dead relatives. Gone was the high-society columnist, replaced by a reporter with a newfound moral sensibility who saw in the misery of Chechnya a story that she would devote the remainder of her life to telling.

The anecdote that Gould relates is cer-

---

* Gould, Terry. *Marked for Death: Dying for the Story in the World's Most Dangerous Places*. Berkeley: Counterpoint, 2009.

tainly a dramatic moment in the life of a journalist that had many other dramatic moments to come. While undoubtedly important in the arc of her career, epiphanies do not arise by chance, popping up de novo in a vacuum without surrounding context. At the time, Politkovskaya's seventeen-year marriage was unraveling, which suggested to Gannushkina that she was open to change, looking elsewhere for meaning in her life. Perhaps there is some validity to this speculation, but motivation with a Politkovskaya-like intensity is likely to have a more complex origin as we shall see. Be that as it may, what is known with greater certainty is that Politkovskaya's shift to investigative journalist dates from the summer of 1996.

Politkovskaya's humanitarian awakening from here on follows a clear timeline. The First Chechen War ended in an uneasy peace that same year, leaving a lot of widows, orphans, and refugees. The war's harsh legacy, which she unwittingly stumbled upon when she entered the office of Civil Assistance, sensitized her to the vio-

lence and extreme brutality still to come.

The year 1999 was auspicious for Politkovskaya for a number of reasons. Her troubled marriage finally ended, and she left *Obshchaya Gazeta* for *Novaya Gazeta*. The twice-weekly liberal leaning tabloid with a circulation of 100,000 was a good fit for her. The paper had received financial support from Mikhail Gorbachev and was entirely owned by the journalists who worked there, ensuring its independence from outside interference. The year also saw the start of the Second Chechen War and the appointment of one Vladimir Putin—head of the Federal Security Service (FSB) that had succeeded the Soviet-era KGB—as prime minister by President Yeltsin. Putin was charged with subduing the rebellious Chechens.

A prelude to the Second Chechen War was the invasion of the neighboring Russian region of Dagestan by Chechen Islamist fighters intent on establishing an independent Islamic state. Soon after hostilities began, Dmitry Muratov, *Novaya Gazeta*'s editor, sent Politkovskaya to

Dagestan to report on the situation. From the very beginning, she focused on the refugees displaced by war and the indifference of the Russian military and political establishment to their plight.

During this period, three bomb attacks within Russia targeted apartment blocks, killing over three hundred people. Chechen separatists were blamed, but the evidence pointed toward the FSB, whose presumed intent was to arouse anti-Chechen sentiment. Russian tanks duly rolled across the border into Chechnya on October 1, 1999, prefaced by an aerial attack on the capital Grozny and Putin's infamous promise to the Russian people to "corner the bandits in the shithouse and wipe them out."

The Second Chechen War gave Anna Politkovskaya her cause célèbre. Time and again, she exposed the gross human rights abuses perpetrated by the Russian military and the FSB; the unlawful detentions, extrajudicial killings of civilian and combatants, the people who "disappeared," and the widespread torture and rape as instruments of terror. She named individual Russian officers, calling them out publicly for their transgressions, a particularly provocative act given their power to exact revenge in lawless Chechnya and an increasing perilous Russia. She lambasted her fellow Russian citizens for their apathy to horrors that were being committed in Chechnya by their army. Her fellow journalists were not spared her ire—she criticized them, too, for what she saw as their reticence in reporting from the front lines of the conflict notwithstanding the extreme hazards that this entailed. And running as a constant, unwavering thread through all her reportage was her excoriating opinion of the man she viewed as the architect of all this misfortune, Vladimir Putin, who had by now succeeded Yeltsin as president.

Politkovskaya blurred the margins between journalism and advocacy in her coverage of the plight of civilians in the Chechen war. They saw her as their champion and trusted her. Her sympathy for them and her exposé of Russian war atrocities made for some dangerous enemies.

On February 21, 2001, she went missing in Chechnya when she was detained by the Russian army, beaten, threatened with rape, poisoned, and subjected to a mock execution. She was only saved by the intervention of a former army officer now working for *Novaya Gazeta*, Major Ismailov, who used his military contacts to intervene on her behalf. She was poisoned again on September 1, 2004, on board an Aeroflot flight to Ossetia in the north Caucasus region of Russia to prevent her covering the takeover of a school in the town of Beslan by Chechen extremists. She was in the hospital when the botched rescue attempt left 333 people dead, including 186 children. That same year, she was openly threatened by Ramzan Kadyrov, prime minister and later president of Chechnya, a Putin acolyte. Threats from Kadyrov were typically followed by a bullet, but this never saw off Politkovskaya. In a subsequent interview with Radio Liberty, she called him the "Chechen Stalin of our days."

None of the intimidation deterred her. She covered the war with a relentless, obsessive intensity, making forty-eight trips to the country in seven years. Even after losing her press access to Chechnya, she would slip across the border in the trunk of a car or disguised as a peasant. She was in the capital, Grozny, when the city was pulverized into rubble. She rejected the repeated, desperate entreaties of her children, editor, colleagues, and friends to stay out of the country and tone down her eviscerating criticism of the army and Putin.

The murder of Politkovskaya on October 7, 2006, would not have come as a complete surprise to those who knew how close she sailed to a lethal wind. But it profoundly shocked them nevertheless. In a country rife with assassinations, her violent death aroused revulsion. It also begged the question: what drove her so hard to pursue a story that came with a death sentence?

"Words can save lives," Politkovskaya is reported to have said. This belief clearly motivated her despite the painful irony, surely not lost on her, that these very same words doomed her.

Another explanation for her headlong pursuit of the story despite the fatal consequences, is that the trauma she suffered along the way made her behavior reckless. Indeed, one of the diagnostic criteria for posttraumatic stress disorder is just this: "reckless or self-destructive behavior."

A third possibility is that Politkovskaya's unwavering commitment to her work was indicative not only of remarkable courage—more so as this overrode great fear—but also of an extreme rigidity in her personality. Much as colleagues admired her, they could find her trying. She was uncompromising and inflexible in her opinions, actions, and wants, and she expected everyone to conform to these, as well. If they did not, they were berated and discarded. Brave, good, and courageous people who were just as appalled by the horrors perpetrated in Chechnya and the suborning of the rule of law in Putin's Russia were not spared this treatment, and it bemused and hurt them. This characterological inflexibility perhaps meant she had only one way of reporting on Chechnya.

There is, however, a fourth factor that must be considered. I believe Terry Gould is spot on when he concluded that Anna Politkovskaya was driven by shame. "Shame for the period during which she hadn't reported the First Chechen War and its atrocities. Shame that twenty-first century Russians could continue to perpetrate such atrocities; that ordinary Russians could support them; that fellow liberal Russians wanted to look the other way; and, finally that Russians had embraced a KBG colonel who was the unconcerned author of those atrocities, one who was herding them gleefully back to the authoritarian state from which they had emerged."

Gould stops here. But we can take his thesis one step further. Shame is one of two primary emotions associated with moral injury. The other is guilt. And if we parse Gould's idea a little more, we see how his language, with reference to "perpetrating" atrocities and being "unconcerned" by them, fits hand-in-glove with a definition of moral injury as the damage done to one's conscience when one perpetrates, witnesses, or fails to prevent acts that transgress one's own values or ethical codes of conduct.

Politkovskaya bore witness but, unlike the vast majority of her fellow citizens, could not keep quiet about what she saw. "Silence is worse," wrote Nietzche, "all truths that are kept silent become poisonous." So it is with moral injury and acts of omission. Anna Politkovskaya knew this. Her extraordinary motivation was an attempt to assuage moral injury. Her courage, at its core, was the product of a profound moral hurt.

The body of Politkovskaya files past mourners. Politkovskaya was assassinated on October 7, 2006.
Her funeral was held in the Troyekurovskoye Cemetery, Moscow, Russia.

About the Author

Anthony Feinstein received his medical degree in South Africa at the University of the Witwatersrand. Thereafter he completed his training in Psychiatry at the Royal Free Hospital in London, England, before training as a neuropsychiatrist at the Institute of Neurology, Queen Square in London. His Master of Philosophy and Ph.D. Degrees were obtained through the University of London, England. He is currently Professor of Psychiatry at the University of Toronto and directs the neuropsychiatry service at Sunnybrook Health Sciences Centre in Toronto. He is a former Chair of the Medical Advisory Committee of the MS Society of Canada.

In 2000-2001 Dr. Feinstein was awarded a Guggenheim Fellowship to study mental health issues in post-apartheid Namibia. This led to the development of that country's first rating scale for psychological distress. Subsequent work in Botswana produced that country's first psychometric measure of emotional distress.

Dr. Feinstein is the author of nine books including *Dangerous Lives: War and the Men and Women Who Report It* (Thomas Allen, Toronto 2003), *Michael Rabin—*

America's Virtuoso Violinist (Amadeus Press, 2005) and *Battle Scarred* (Tafelberg, 2011). His most recent book is *Shooting War* (G Editions, 2018), in which he profiled 18 conflict photographers. In 2012 he produced a documentary, "Under Fire," based on his research of frontline journalists and which received a Peabody Award. His 12-part series for the *Globe and Mail* on this topic was short-listed for a 2016 EPPY award.

Dr. Feinstein lives with his family in Toronto, Canada.

Acknowledgments

I want to thank the 19 journalists who all spoke candidly and at length about their lives and careers. They come from diverse backgrounds encompassing multiple countries, languages and cultures and yet they have the same goals, keeping alive freedom of expression and championing the rights of citizens to know what their governments are up to. These ideals are shared to such an extent one might say that I have written 19 variations on a single theme. What these journalists also have in common is a generosity of spirit—they gave me their time and trust and shared details of experiences that were uplifting but also at times distressing to hear.

My thoughts on moral courage as a primary motivating factor that compels journalists to stand up to harsh, authoritarian governments were first shared with David Walmsley, Editor-in-Chief of the *Globe and Mail* in Canada. Our discussions were framed by events that have undermined the integrity of the media. The spread of fake news, demonization of journalists and manipulation of the media for malign purposes have taken root globally. What better way to push back against these dan-gerous developments than by highlighting the work of journalists who represent the very antithesis of this false narrative. David generously gave me the space and time to develop my ideas and share them in the public domain. In doing so he has brought a much needed focus to the importance of moral injury and its counterweight, moral courage, in his profession.

Clare Vander Meersch was Photo Editor for this book. Her day job is Photo Editor at the *Globe and Mail*. Clare, with her extensive network of contacts, was wonderfully helpful in commissioning the 19 photographers, one for each of the journalists profiled. The selection of images was guided by her deep knowledge of photography and keen eye for the right image to provide a visual accompaniment to the text. I was fortunate indeed to her expertise every step of the way.

There are a number of people who opened doors for me when it came to contacting the journalists I wanted to interview. My thanks go to Joel Simon, former President of the *Committee to Protect Journalists*, and his successor, Jodie Ginsberg, Lauren Jackman at the *Organized Crime and*

Corruption Reporting Project, Caroline Korba and Elise Munoz at the *International Women's Media Foundation*, and Corinne Dufka and Emma Daly at *Human Rights Watch*.

My "Moral Courage" series for the *Globe and Mail*, which forms the basis for this book, touched a number of readers and I thank those who took the time to write to me. My email inbox would light up after an article was published. The messages conveyed admiration for the journalists, appreciation for their work, offers to donate money to organizations that support journalists and questions for me about moral injury and moral courage.

It must be said that there was the occasional message that contained a diatribe, the sender's hostility to a particular country alighting on the journalist instead. Such misplaced fury is one of the unavoidable realities of social media. But these rare, angry voices were overridden by the many emails expressing admiration for these journalists' work. The good outweighed the bad. The moral courage of the 19 journalists won the day.

My work on moral injury and moral courage is a continuation of a line of research that began with a Guggenheim Fellowship in 2000. In the years that followed, my research came to the attention of David Thomson, Chairman of *Thomson Reuters*. His enthusiasm and support for the subject of good journalism and the emotional health of journalists have been invaluable in shepherding my ideas and plans to fruition. This book is testimony to that.

I am fortunate in having Marta Hallett as my publisher. Marta has a rare elixir, part intense passion for her work, part personal warmth, that transforms the rocky journey from idea to the printed page into a process that is actually enjoyable.

And now I come to family. Thanking them always seems somehow inadequate, falling miserably short of what I am trying to convey. So let me approach this from a slightly different angle. My work is nourished by Kally and Pippa, Saul and Clarrie. They provide the bedrock from which everything flows.

Profile Photography Credits

Gwen Lister
Photographs copyright © Charlie Shoemaker

Abdul Mujeeb Khalvatgar
Photographs copyright © Alana Paterson and
Nai Supporting Open Media in Afghanistan

Larysa Shchyrakova
Photographs copyright © Alfredo Bosco

Mohammad Mosaed
Photographs copyright © Louie Palu

Neha Dixit
Photographs copyright © Sahiba Chawdhary

David Frenkel
Photographs copyright © Mary Gelman

Victoria Razo and Felix Marquez
Photographs copyright © Victoria Razo and
Felix Marquez

Kishore
Photographs copyright © Shahidul
Alam/Drik

Yakeen Bido
Photographs copyright © Aref Tammawi

Can Dündar
Photographs copyright © Mustafah Abdulaziz;

Ozan Kose/AFP/Getty Images and Can Erok/
Cumhuriyet Newspaper via Getty Images.

Khadija Ismayilova
Photographs copyright © Sitara Ibrahimbayli

Hopewell Rugoho-Chin'ono
Photographs copyright
© Cynthia R. Matonhodze

Pavla Holcová
Photographs copyright © Lenka Klicperová

Stevan Dojčinović
Photographs copyright © Martyn Aim

Mwape Kumwenda
Photographs copyright © Edith Sampa Chiliboy

Aye Chan Naing
Photographs copyright © Andrea Gjestvang

Cándido Figueredo Ruíz
Photographs copyright © Ryan Collerd

Anna Politkovskaya
Photographs copyright © *Novaya Gazeta*/Epsi-
lon/Getty Images; Jens Schlueter/DDP/AFP/
via Getty Images; and Justin Jin (funeral image)

Author Anthony Feinstein
Photograph copyright © Rita Leistner

Index